ENTERTAINING
WITH
APPETIZERS

CONTENTS

ANOTHER BEST-SELLING VOLUME FROM HPBooks®
Publisher: Rick Bailey; Executive Editor: Randy Summerlin
Editorial Director: Elaine R. Woodard; Editor: Jeanette P. Egan
Art Director: Don Burton; Book Assembly: Paul Fitzgerald
Production Manager: Cindy J. Coatsworth; Typography: Michelle Carter
Director of Manufacturing: Anthony B. Narducci

Published by HPBooks
A Division of HPBooks, Inc.
P.O. Box 5367, Tucson, AZ 85703   602/888-2150
ISBN 0-89586-473-8
Library of Congress Catalog Card Number 86-80778
©1986 HPBooks, Inc.   Printed in the U.S.A.
1st Printing

Portions of this book originally published as:
The Best of Sainsbury's Entertaining ©1985 Cathay Books; Sweet Temptations, Cooking for
Two, French Cooking, Poultry and Game, Cheesecakes, Salads & Snacks, Make More of
Vegetables, Delicious Fish Dishes, Cooking for Special Occasions ©1982, 1981, 1979, 1978
Hennerwood Publications Limited

Cover Photo: Selection of Open Face Sandwiches, page 63

INTRODUCTION

Appetizers include spicy dips, tiny sandwiches, cold and hot soups, crunchy salads, warm quiches and much more. Appetizers can be served for a cocktail party, as substitutes for a meal, as snacks or as the first course for a meal. The type and number of appetizers will depend on the occasion.

STARTERS

The first course of a meal is designed to stimulate the appetite. Vegetables, whether in a soup or served on their own, such as buttered asparagus, are an excellent choice for this as they are neither too rich nor too filling. Soups and salads are often used as starters for a meal. Always choose the recipe carefully, keeping in mind that it should make a pleasant contrast in flavor and texture to the following courses. The appetizer should complement the rest of the menu. Don't repeat flavors of the appetizer in other courses.

Some excellent starters include dishes, such as Cucumber Soup, Bell-Pepper & Salami Salad, Stuffed Smoked-Salmon Rolls or Stuffed Pears. If the main dish is light, choose a more substantial appetizer. However, if the main dish is hearty, choose a light, delicate starter, such as a light soup. Starters should be presented attractively; choose simple garnishes and attractive serving dishes.

APPETIZERS FOR BUFFETS

A small buffet appetizer party for around 20 people is the ideal way to informally entertain. Wonderfully relaxed, appetizer parties are the almost anything goes kind of party. The food can be deliciously simple or sumptuously extravagant depending upon your budget and available time.

If you don't have room for a sit-down meal, a buffet is ideal. Another advantage of these parties is that you can entertain large groups of people. Your guests can help themselves to food and eat as little or as much as they like. Most of the preparation can be done in advance, allowing you to enjoy the party too. Good planning is still a must, but once plentiful supplies of plates, napkins, silverware and food have been laid out there is little more to do than occasionally check in case anything runs low.

When planning the menu for your buffet party, choose dishes that allow guests to help themselves. Also select food that can be eaten easily with the fingers or a fork, as most of the guests will probably be standing to eat, and may have to hold a glass of wine or other beverage at the same time.

Try to keep individual items as small as possible so that they can be eaten in one or two bites, but provide plates and forks in case some of the guests prefer not to eat with their fingers.

Stuffed items, such as cucumber pieces, eggs, small tomatoes, celery pieces and mushrooms, look both attractive and colorful when arranged on platters for a buffet table. Guests can easily help themselves to foods such as these.

Some of the foods in the chapter for buffets, such as pâtés and mousses, can be cut into individual slices and served as starters. Also many of the individual appetizers in the chapter on Canapés & Hors d'Oeuvres can be used for a buffet appetizer party, such as an open house.

If you are having a buffet or open house, advance planning is important to ensure that the party will be a success. It is essential to plan your menu several days before the party. When you have decided on the number of guests to be invited—and they have accepted the invitations—you can determine the quantities needed. Each recipe has the number of servings at the bottom of the method. This helps determine how many dishes you will need to make for the number of guests that are coming.

CANAPÉS & HORS D'OEUVRES

Canapés are small appetizers that are served on toast, crackers or pastry shells. Ideally, canapés should be small enough to eat in one or two bites. To make canapés, removes crusts from white or whole-wheat bread, toast lightly on both sides and cut slices in halves or quarters. Or cut in small rounds after toasting. If preferred, the canapé base can be made of savory cheese pastry—use the recipe for Cheese Straws. Or use flatbreads and crackers as bases. For an eye-catching spread, combine different shapes, textures and toppings on the same platter.

Hors d'oeuvres are small appetizers that are not

served on bread. They include items, such as stuffed celery, cheese cubes, olives and nuts. They should also be small enough to eat in one or two bites.

Plan on guests eating about six appetizers. Always include some low-calorie appetizers for those guests who are watching their weight! For only two or three guests, one or two different appetizers should be enough. For a larger group, four or five appetizers should be served. Vary the temperature, flavor and texture of the appetizers. If a meal is not being served, the appetizers should be heartier. Small open-face sandwiches or sliced pâté would be ideal. When you invite your guests, let them know the type of party and whether it's only appetizers or appetizers and a meal to follow.

If a meal is being served, limit the number of appetizers and the length of the cocktail hour. Don't fill your guests with appetizers and then sit down to a complete dinner.

BEVERAGES

Beverages are an important part of any party. The easiest way to serve beverages is to have a punch to which guests can help themselves. If you're serving alcoholic punch, also offer a nonalcoholic punch. Wine is an alternative to mixed drinks, and many people today prefer to drink wine. One 750ml bottle of wine contains four to six servings. Include mineral waters and soft drinks for those guests who do not want to drink alcohol. Plan on guests having two or three drinks during a party. You will need extra glasses, because guests may want a new glass when they have another drink. If you're short of drink glasses, there are several good quality clear plastic ones available.

Coffee and tea are appropriate for an open house or an afternoon party. Late afternoon or early evening teas are possible substitutes for a cocktail party. The usual time for tea is between 3:00 and 5:00 pm. A tea can be as simple or elaborate as you wish to make it. Often both coffee and tea are served. A simple cake and one or two dainty sandwiches may be enough. For a special tea, you will want to use your finest tea service and plan on a wider selection of foods. In addition to cakes and sandwiches, don't forget to arrange the sugar, lemon slices and milk on a tray for easy serving.

Finishing Touches

The finishing touch for any cocktail is the decoration. You can choose from the simple to the sumptuous. Any of the following can be used effectively to add eye appeal:

- Maraschino cherries, red or green.
- Lemon, lime, orange and pineapple slices.
- Green olives, plain or stuffed for martinis.
- Citrus peel twists to place on the side of the glass and citrus peel spirals for inside drinks.
- Celery leaves or stalks, cucumber peel and mint sprigs.
- Petite parasol umbrellas in a multitude of colors and designs.
- Melon wedges to position on the glass rim.
- Plain and colored sugar for frosting glass rims.
- Spices, such as cinnamon and nutmeg, for tops of drinks.

Drinks

A few cleverly concocted drinks can get a party off to a good start. They invite comment and stimulate conversation. Always provide nonalcoholic beverages for guests who do not drink.

It is important to measure ingredients accurately. A jigger in these recipes refers to a standard jigger of 1-1/2 ounces or 3 tablespoons. A jigger is worth buying if you serve cocktails regularly. To improvise, use a standard liqueur glass which holds about 1 ounce or a standard tablespoon.

SWEET TEMPTATIONS

It's always fun to end a party with a few well chosen treats. Select dessert items that can be eaten in one or two bites. Candies, cookies and small cakes are perfect. Teas usually include one or more sweets, such as petits fours. Arrange your bite-size treats in small paper cups, or place them directly on a tray or plate.

SERVING APPETIZERS

Decide on the type of appetizers to be served. If several appetizers are served, special utensils and equipment may be needed. If food is to be served hot, warming trays, chafing dishes or fondue pots will be needed. Small electric skillets or slow cookers are also useful for keeping food hot.

Food that must be kept chilled can be placed in a bowl nestled in a bed of ice cubes in a deep pan or larger bowl. The ice and pan can be covered with lettuce leaves or other garnishes to make it more pleasing. Make sure that the ice container does not leak as the ice melts. If heavy serving pieces are chilled before arranging the food, they will keep food cool for some time. In addition, plan some items that can be served at room temperature.

For added confidence, do a trial run the day before the party. Arrange serving equipment on the table to make sure everything fits and looks attractive. For a large party, arrange food and beverages in more than one location. This prevents grouping around the food table.

Arrange food attractively on the serving plates and trays. Don't crowd food on plates. It's often better to have two small trays than one large tray. When the tray is almost empty, replace it with a fresh tray. This keeps the table neater.

Don't forget a centerpiece for your table. If the party has an ethnic theme, choose an appropriate basket or carving to add interest and authenticity. Flowers are always appropriate as a centerpiece, but choose them carefully. As a rule, flowers with a pronounced fragrance should not be on a table with food.

Garnish the food to make it more appealing. Garnishes need not be elaborate; simple parsley sprigs, tomato wedges and lemon slices may be enough. If possible, make garnishes ahead of time.

Now that all the planning and preparation is finished, relax, welcome your guests and enjoy your party!

MENUS

Here are some suggested menus for ideas on combining foods. Remember to have variety in flavor, color, texture and temperature and include some foods that can be made ahead. The amount of food will vary, depending on appetite, the time of the party and whether a meal is also being served. The amounts listed below can be used as general guidelines for appetizer parties that do not precede meals.

Appetizers for 20

- 1 recipe Chicken & Mushroom Vol-au-Vents
- 2 recipes Pimento-Cream Cheese Spread on crackers
- 2 recipes Bacon-Cream Cheese Spread on crackers
- 1-1/2 recipes Celery Boats
- 1-1/2 recipes Cucumber Canoes
- 2 recipes Crudités
- 1 recipe Salted Nuts

Christmas Open House for 50

- 1 recipe Tuna & Parmesan Puffs
- 4 recipes Deviled Crab Dip with Vegetables
- 3 recipes Date-Cream Cheese Spread on crackers or nut bread
- 2 recipes Blue-Cheese Mousse with assorted crackers
- 3 recipes Cheese Straws
- 2 recipes Deviled Nuts
- 2 recipes Truffles
- 2 recipes Petits Fours
- 2 recipes Claret Punch
- Coffee and tea

Small Garden Wedding for 25

- 3 recipes Mushroom & Seafood Italienne
- 2 recipes Summer Mousse with Assorted Crackers
- 2 recipes Herbed Chicken Loaf
- 4 recipes Curried Potato Salad
- 2 recipes Orange & Endive Salad
- Wedding cake
- 2 recipes Peppermint Creams
- 3 recipes Spiced Almonds
- 2 recipes Champagne Punch
- Coffee and tea

Afternoon Tea for 12

- Small Sandwiches filled with 1 recipe Salmon Spread
- Small Sandwiches filled with 1 recipe Cucumber-Cream Cheese Spread
- 1/2 recipe Stuffed Dates
- 1/2 recipe Printainiers
- Coffee and tea

Appetizers for 10

- 1 recipe Marinated Mushrooms
- 1 recipe Shrimp-Filled Pastries
- 1 recipe Stuffed Tomatoes
- 1 recipe Cheese Kabobs

Grazing Party for 20

- 1 recipe Country-Style Chicken Pâté
- 2 recipes Smoked-Salmon Flan
- 1 recipe Ham Rolls
- 2 recipes Seafood Risotto
- 4 recipes Asparagus with Butter
- 4 recipes Tomato & Basil Salad
- 2 recipes Chinese Salad
- Assorted breads and crackers

STARTERS

Smoked-Salmon Flan

Pastry:
1-1/2 cups all-purpose flour
1/2 teaspoon salt
1/2 cup vegetable shortening
3 to 4 tablespoons ice water

Smoked-Salmon Filling:
6 oz. smoked-salmon pieces
2 tablespoons chopped fresh chives or parsley
3 eggs
Salt to taste
Freshly ground pepper to taste
1/2 pint half and half (1 cup)
1/2 cup milk

---

1. To make pastry, in a medium bowl, combine flour and salt. With a pastry blender or 2 knives, cut in shortening until mixture resembles coarse crumbs.
2. Sprinkle with 3 tablespoons water; toss with a fork until mixture holds together, adding more water if necessary. Gather dough into a flattened ball. Wrap in plastic wrap or waxed paper; refrigerate 30 minutes.
3. Preheat oven to 400F (205C). On a lightly floured board, roll out dough into an 11-inch circle. Use to line a 9- or 10-inch pie pan or quiche pan. Crimp and flute edge if desired; prick bottom lightly with a fork. Line pastry with foil; fill with pie weights or dried beans.
4. Bake in preheated oven 15 minutes. Remove foil and pie weights or beans; bake 5 to 8 minutes or until golden brown. Set aside to cool.
5. Reduce oven temperature to 375F (190C). Chop salmon; arrange in bottom of cooled pie shell. Sprinkle with chives or parsley. In a medium bowl, beat eggs, salt and pepper, half and half and milk until combined; pour into pie shell.
6. Bake in preheated oven 35 to 45 minutes or until puffed and top is golden brown. Cool in pan on a wire rack 15 minutes; serve warm. Makes 6 servings.

Variation
Flan can be baked in individual flan pans. Reduce cooking time to about 20 minutes.

Seafood Risotto

2 tablespoons butter or margarine
1 large onion, chopped
1-1/4 cups long-grain white rice
2-1/2 cups fish or chicken stock
1 teaspoon dried dill
Salt to taste
Fresh ground pepper
8 oz. sole fillets, skinned
4 oz. peeled shrimp
4 oz. mushrooms, sliced
1 cup cooked or canned peas

To garnish:
Pimento strips
Few cooked mussels

---

1. Melt butter or margarine in a medium saucepan. Add onion; sauté until soft, stirring occasionally. Add rice; cook 1 to 2 minutes, stirring well. Stir in stock, dill, salt and pepper. Bring to a boil. Reduce heat. Cover and simmer 20 minutes.
2. Cut fish into narrow strips; add fish strips, shrimp and mushrooms to rice mixture. Stir well, cover and simmer about 10 minutes or until fish turns from transparent to opaque, stirring occasionally. Add more boiling stock, if necessary.
3. Stir in peas; heat through. Spoon into 4 to 6 individual dishes; top with pimento and mussels. Serve hot. Makes 4 to 6 servings.

Clockwise from left: Seafood Risotto; Smoked-Salmon Flan; Mussels Marinière, page 11

Crispy Cheese & Crab Bites

1/2 cup butter or margarine
3/4 cup all-purpose flour
3 cups milk
Salt to taste
Freshly ground pepper to taste
Dash of freshly grated nutmeg
3 cups shredded Swiss cheese (12 oz.)
1/4 cup grated Parmesan cheese (3/4 oz.)
2 (6-oz.) pkgs. frozen crabmeat, thawed, drained
4 egg yolks, beaten
2 eggs
1/4 cup milk
About 2 cups fresh bread crumbs
Vegetable oil

To garnish:
Fried parsley sprigs

1. Melt butter or margarine in a medium saucepan. Stir in flour; cook 2 minutes, stirring. Gradually stir in 3 cups milk. Bring to a boil, stirring constantly. Season with salt, pepper and nutmeg. Add cheeses; stir until melted.
2. Remove mixture from heat; stir in crabmeat and egg yolks. Spread mixture 1/2-inch thick in a shallow baking pan. Cover with foil; refrigerate 3 to 4 hours.
3. Cut chilled mixture into rectangles, about 1-1/2 inches long. In a shallow bowl, beat eggs and 1/4 cup milk. Dip cheese rectangles into egg mixture, then into bread crumbs to coat evenly.
4. Heat 3 inches oil in a deep-fryer or heavy pan to 375F (190C) or until a 1-inch cube turns golden brown in 50 seconds. Add coated rectangles in batches; fry until crisp and golden. Drain on paper towels. Keep hot in the oven until ready to serve. Garnish with parsley before serving. Makes about 12 servings.

Mushroom & Seafood Italienne

1 lb. mushrooms, thinly sliced
1/4 cup olive oil
1/4 cup lemon or lime juice
1 garlic clove, crushed
2 teaspoons chopped parsley
Freshly ground pepper to taste
Salt to taste
8 sea scallops
1/2 cup dry white wine
2 parsley sprigs
1/2 small onion
Strip of lemon peel
8 oz. peeled, cooked shrimp
Few lettuce leaves

To garnish:
Parsley sprigs
Lime or lemon wedges

1. In a medium bowl, combine mushrooms, olive oil and lemon or lime juice. Sprinkle with garlic, chopped parsley, pepper and salt. Toss to combine; cover and let stand 30 minutes.
2. Slice each scallop into 2 or 3 slices; set aside. Combine wine, parsley sprigs, onion and lemon peel in a medium saucepan; bring to a boil. Add scallops; cook 2 minutes.
3. Using a slotted spoon, lift out cooked scallops. Add cooked scallops and shrimp to mushroom mixture. Discard cooking liquid. Mushroom mixture can be covered and refrigerated up to 6 hours.
4. To serve, arrange lettuce leaves in individual serving dishes; spoon mushroom mixture over lettuce. Garnish with parsley and lime or lemon wedges. Makes 8 to 12 servings.

Mussels

Grown and harvested commercially, these shellfish are now available all year in U.S. markets. Use within a day of purchasing. Do not refrigerate in plastic bags or the mussels will suffocate and begin to spoil. Scrub shells under cold, running water. Pull off and discard the tough brown beard. Discard any opened shells.

Mussels Marinière

Photo on page 9.

3 lbs. mussels in shells
1/4 cup butter or margarine
1 large onion, very finely chopped
1 garlic clove, minced
2 cups white wine
Salt to taste
Freshly ground pepper to taste
1 bay leaf
1 parsley sprig
1 thyme sprig
4 teaspoons all-purpose flour
2 to 3 tablespoons chopped parsley

1. Scrub mussels with a brush to remove all dirt. Discard any that are broken or do not close when given a sharp tap; set aside.
2. Melt 3 tablespoons butter or margarine in a large pot. Add onion and garlic; sauté until soft, about 5 minutes. Add wine, salt, pepper, bay leaf, parsley and thyme. Reduce heat; simmer 2 minutes.
3. Add mussels, a few at a time, shaking well until all are added to the pan. Cover and simmer 4 to 6 minutes or until mussels open. Discard any which do not open. Place mussels in a bowl; keep warm. Discard bay leaf, parsley sprig and thyme sprig.
4. In a small bowl, mix remaining 1 tablespoon butter or margarine and flour to make a paste; whisk into cooking liquid. Stir in chopped parsley; simmer 2 minutes, stirring. Pour over mussels; serve hot. Makes 4 servings.

Crab & Bacon Rolls

1 (6-oz.) pkg. frozen crabmeat, thawed, drained
1 egg, beaten
1-1/2 cups fresh bread crumbs
About 1/2 cup tomato juice
1 teaspoon dried leaf basil
1 teaspoon chopped parsley
Salt to taste
Freshly ground pepper to taste
12 bacon slices

To garnish:
Tomato wedges
Watercress sprigs

1. Position oven rack about 4 to 6 inches below heat source. Preheat broiler.
2. With your fingertips, pick through crabmeat, discarding bits of shell and cartilage. In a medium bowl, combine crabmeat, egg, bread crumbs and enough tomato juice to bind. Stir in basil, parsley, salt and pepper.
3. Shape mixture into 12 rolls, about 3 inches long. Wrap 1 bacon slice around each 1, then secure with a wooden pick. Place on a rack over a broiler pan.
4. Broil until bacon is crisp, turning frequently. Arrange on a hot serving dish; garnish with tomatoes and watercress. Makes 12 appetizers.

Left to right: Mushrooms & Seafood Italienne, Crispy Cheese & Crab Bites

Stuffed Smoked-Salmon Rolls

Photo on page 31.

1 teaspoon gelatin powder
3 tablespoons lemon juice
1 tablespoon water
1 (8-oz.) pkg. cream cheese, room temperature
3 green onions, finely chopped
2 tablespoons chopped chives
1/4 cup mayonnaise or whipping cream, lightly
  whipped
Salt to taste
Freshly ground white pepper to taste
8 (1-oz.) thin slices smoked salmon

To serve:
2 lemons, cut into wedges
Green onions

1. In a small saucepan, combine gelatin, lemon juice and water. Let stand 3 minutes. Stir over low heat until gelatin dissolves. Cool slightly.
2. Meanwhile, in a medium bowl, beat cheese until soft. Beat in green onions and chives. Beat in mayonnaise or whipping cream, salt and pepper. Fold in gelatin mixture until evenly blended. Cover and refrigerate until mixture is firm, but not set.
3. Lay salmon slices flat on a work surface. Divide cheese mixture equally among them, placing cheese mixture on 1 end of each slice. Roll salmon to enclose filling.
4. Arrange salmon rolls on a platter; cover and refrigerate at least 4 hours or up to 8 hours. Garnish with lemon slices and green onions. Serve chilled. Makes 4 servings.

Grapefruit-Stuffed Avocados

Minted Grape & Melon Cocktail

Minted Grape & Melon Cocktail

2 small honeydew melons
Few fresh mint leaves
8 to 12 oz. grapes, halved, seeded

To garnish:
Mint sprigs

1. Cut melons in half; remove seeds. Crush a few mint leaves; place into melon centers. Add grapes.
2. Cover and refrigerate about 1 hour before serving. Garnish with mint sprigs. Makes 4 servings.

Grapefruit-Stuffed Avocados

1 large grapefruit
2 ripe avocados, halved, pitted
6 tablespoons French Dressing, page 25

To garnish:
Fresh mint or parsley sprigs

1. Peel grapefruit, removing skin and bitter, white pith. Cut peeled grapefruit into sections. Cut large sections in half. Place an avocado half in each of 4 dishes, cut-sides up.
2. Drizzle cut surfaces of avocados with a little dressing to prevent browning. Put about 1 tablespoon dressing into each avocado half. Arrange grapefruit in avocado centers. Garnish with mint or parsley sprigs. Makes 4 servings.

Greek-Style Mushrooms

1/4 cup vegetable oil
2 garlic cloves, crushed
1 small onion, finely chopped
2 bay leaves
1 thyme sprig
1 rosemary sprig
2 parsley sprigs
2/3 cup dry white wine
4 to 6 black peppercorns
12 coriander seeds
1-1/2 lbs. button mushrooms
Salt to taste

To garnish:
Chopped parsley

Serve with French bread or whole-wheat rolls.

1. Heat oil in a medium saucepan. Add garlic and onion; cook until soft but not browned, 5 minutes, stirring occasionally. Add bay leaves, thyme, rosemary, parsley and wine. Bring to a boil. Reduce heat and simmer 2 minutes. Add peppercorns, coriander seeds, mushrooms and salt.
2. Toss mushrooms in wine sauce until well coated. Transfer to a stainless steel bowl. Cover and refrigerate until chilled, 3 to 4 hours, stirring occasionally.
3. To serve, transfer to a serving bowl with a slotted spoon, discarding marinade. Sprinkle with chopped parsley. Makes 6 servings.

Crispy Mushrooms with Herb & Garlic Mayonnaise

Herb & Garlic Mayonnaise:
1/2 cup mayonnaise
2 garlic cloves, crushed
2 tablespoons chopped parsley
1 tablespoon chopped basil

Batter:
3/4 cup all-purpose flour
Pinch of salt
1 tablespoon vegetable oil
1/2 cup water
2 egg whites

1 lb. button mushrooms
Vegetable oil

---

1. To prepare mayonnaise, combine all ingredients in a small bowl; pour into a serving bowl. Cover and refrigerate while preparing mushrooms.
2. To make batter, sift flour and salt into a medium bowl. Gradually beat in oil and water. Beat egg whites until stiff but not dry; fold into batter.
3. Drop mushrooms into batter. Heat 3 inches oil in a large saucepan or deep-fryer to 375F (190C) or until a 1-inch bread cube turns golden brown in 50 seconds. Lift mushrooms from batter to oil with a slotted spoon. Deep-fry mushrooms in batches until golden brown.
4. Drain on paper towels; keep hot. Serve with mayonnaise. Makes 4 to 6 servings.

Left to right: Marinated Mushrooms, Crispy Mushrooms with Herb & Garlic Mayonnaise

Stuffed Pears

1/2 (8-oz.) pkg. cream cheese, room temperature
1 tablespoon chopped chives
2 teaspoons chopped parsley
1/4 cup chopped walnuts
1 apple, peeled, cored, grated
2 teaspoons lemon juice
1 head Belgian endive
4 large pears
Lemon juice
4 to 8 slices prosciutto

1. In a small bowl, beat cream cheese until soft. Stir in chives, parsley and nuts. Fold in apple and lemon juice.
2. Arrange endive on 4 to 8 individual serving plates. Peel, halve and core pears. Brush pears with lemon juice.
3. Spoon filling into pear centers; arrange 1 to 2 halves on each plate. Roll up ham slices; arrange 1 slice on each serving. Serve immediately. Makes 4 to 8 servings.

Prosciutto with Figs & Melon

1 honeydew melon, cut into 6 wedges
18 thin slices prosciutto
12 ripe figs

1. Starting at 1 end of melon wedge, loosen melon flesh from skin by running a knife between flesh and skin. Cut melon flesh crosswise into about 8 slices.
2. Arrange ham on 6 individual plates; top with melon. Remove stem ends from figs. Cut figs into sections, from stem end nearly through to large end. Peel back skin; arrange 2 figs on each plate. Makes 6 servings.

Guacamole

2 ripe avocados
1 garlic clove, crushed
1/2 onion, chopped
1 tablespoon lime juice
2 drops hot-pepper sauce
4 medium tomatoes, peeled, seeded, chopped
2 tablespoons chopped parsley
Salt to taste
Freshly ground pepper to taste
1 teaspoon chili powder

To garnish:
Lime slices

Serve with crisp tortilla chips or thin toast slices.

1. Peel, halve and pit avocados. Process avocados, garlic, onion, lime juice, hot-pepper sauce, tomatoes and parsley until smooth in a blender or food processor fitted with the steel blade.
2. Season with salt and pepper; add chili powder. Process until combined. Spoon into a serving dish. Garnish with lime slices. Makes 4 to 6 servings.

Top to bottom: Stuffed Pears, Prosciutto with Figs & Melon, Guacamole

Asparagus with Butter

1 lb. asparagus
Salt to taste
1/4 cup butter or margarine, melted

Use a wide, not too shallow pan to cook asparagus. A deep-fryer with a wire basket or an electric skillet is ideal.

1. Wash asparagus stalks thoroughly under cold, running water, taking care not to damage delicate tops. Trim off woody ends, cutting all stalks to the same length.
2. Place asparagus in a wire basket or tie into 2 bundles so they they can be easily lifted. Add asparagus and salt to boiling water. Reduce heat; simmer about 15 minutes or until tender. Cooking time depends on the size of the stalks.
3. Drain asparagus well; untie if necessary. Serve with melted butter or margarine. Makes 3 to 4 servings.

Variation
Mix 1 finely chopped hard-cooked egg and 1 tablespoon chopped fresh parsley into melted butter before serving.

Artichokes with Butter

4 artichokes
2 tablespoons lemon juice or vinegar
1/4 cup butter or margarine, melted
Salt to taste

Serve artichokes either hot or cold with melted butter or margarine or Hollandaise Sauce.

1. Pull off lower leaves. Trim stalks to about 1 inch or less. Cut off top 1/4 of artichokes. Trim tips of leaves. Using a small, sharp-edged spoon, scrape out and discard tender cone of leaves in center and the fuzzy center. Keep prepared artichokes in a bowl of cold water with 1 tablespoon lemon juice or vinegar to prevent discoloring.
2. Add 3 inches water to a large pan; add salt. Bring to a boil. Add 1 tablespoon lemon juice or vinegar. Add artichokes; cook 30 to 40 minutes or until a leaf near center will pull off easily.
3. Drain artichokes upside down a few minutes. Serve with butter or margarine and finger bowls of warm water.
4. To eat an artichoke, strip away a leaf, then, holding it in your fingers, dip it into the selected sauce. Draw it lightly through your teeth to remove the tender part. Leave the inedible piece on the side of your plate. Continue in this way until you reach the heart of the artichoke, scrape away choke if it has not already been removed and eat the heart with a knife and fork. Makes 4 servings.

Left to right: Asparagus with Butter, Artichokes with Butter, Hollandaise Sauce, Tartar Sauce

Hollandaise Sauce

3 tablespoons white-wine vinegar
6 peppercorns
1 small bay leaf
2 tablespoons water
3 egg yolks
3/4 cup butter, melted
Salt to taste
Lemon juice to taste

Try this rich buttery sauce with fresh asparagus instead of the traditional melted butter. Serve warm, not hot.

1. Boil vinegar, peppercorns and bay leaf in a small saucepan until liquid is reduced to one-third. Strain and discard bay leaf and peppercorns. Set reduced liquid aside.
2. Place bottom of a double boiler containing water over medium-low heat; bring water to a simmer. Reduce heat to low. Add reduced liquid, water and egg yolks to top of double boiler; place over simmering water. Whisk rapidly. Continue whisking as egg mixture thickens and lightens in color, 7 to 8 minutes.
3. Gradually beat in butter to make a thick sauce. Add salt and lemon juice. Remove from heat; keep warm until served. Makes about 1 cup.

Tartar Sauce

1 teaspoon chopped parsley
1/2 teaspoon dried leaf tarragon
1 teaspoon chopped sweet dill pickle
1 teaspoon chopped capers
1/2 cup mayonnaise

1. In a small bowl, combine parsley, tarragon, pickle, capers and mayonnaise.
2. Cover and refrigerate until served or up to 3 days. Makes about 1/2 cup.

Zucchini & Chive Salad

2 medium zucchini
1 tablespoon olive oil
2 tablespoons lemon juice
Large pinch of salt
Freshly ground pepper to taste
1 tablespoon chopped chives

1. In a medium saucepan, cook zucchini in lightly salted boiling water 5 minutes. Drain and rinse in cold water. Cut zucchini crosswise into 1/2-inch slices; place in a shallow serving dish.
2. In a small bowl, whisk oil, lemon juice, salt and pepper until combined; pour over zucchini. Sprinkle with chopped chives. Cover and refrigerate about 30 minutes before serving. Makes 4 servings.

Swedish Potato Salad

1-1/2 lbs. small new potatoes
Salt to taste
2 tablespoons French dressing, page 25
4 oz. cooked beets, diced
1 large dill pickle, diced
5 tablespoons Yogurt Dressing, page 25

To garnish:
1 tablespoon chopped fresh dill

1. Scrub potatoes; leave skins on. Cook in boiling salted water until tender; drain well. In a medium bowl, combine French Dressing and warm potatoes. Cool to room temperature.
2. Add beets, pickle and Yogurt Dressing. Mix well; transfer to a salad bowl. Sprinkle with dill. Makes 6 servings.

Potato & Radish Vinaigrette

1 lb. small new potatoes
Salt to taste
1/4 cup Vinaigrette Dressing, page 25
4 green onions, sliced
1 bunch of radishes, thinly sliced

1. Scrub potatoes; leave skins on. Cook in boiling salted water until tender; drain well. In a medium bowl, combine dressing and warm potatoes. Cool to room temperature.
2. Add green onions and radishes; mix well. Transfer to a salad bowl. Makes 4 servings.

Cabbage & Pepper Salad

1 leek, thinly sliced
1 head of Chinese or napa cabbage, shredded
1 green bell pepper, finely sliced
6 tablespoons Herb Dressing, page 25

1. Separate leek slices into rings. Combine leek rings and cabbage in a medium bowl.
2. Add green pepper and dressing; toss to combine. Transfer to a salad bowl; serve immediately. Makes 6 to 8 servings.

Zucchini & Tomato Salad

2 small zucchini, very thinly sliced
6 tablespoons Garlic Dressing, page 25
6 small tomatoes, sliced
2 oz. pitted ripe olives, halved
1 tablespoon chopped fresh marjoram or 1 teaspoon dried leaf marjoram
1 tablespoon chopped parsley

The very small, young zucchini are the most suitable to use raw in salads. They must be sliced very thinly to allow the flavor of the dressing to be absorbed.

1. Place zucchini in a medium bowl. Add dressing; toss to combine. Cover and refrigerate overnight.
2. Add remaining ingredients; toss to combine. Transfer to a salad bowl. Makes 4 to 6 servings.

Waldorf Salad

1 lb. Red Delicious apples (3 medium)
3 tablespoons lemon juice
1/2 cup mayonnaise
3 celery stalks, chopped
1/2 cup chopped walnuts
1 head of lettuce, separated into leaves

1. Core apples. Thinly slice 1 apple. In a small bowl, toss sliced apple with 1 tablespoon lemon juice; set aside. Dice remaining apples.
2. In a medium bowl, combine remaining 2 tablespoons lemon juice and 1 tablespoon mayonnaise. Add diced apples to lemon-juice mixture; let stand 30 minutes. Add celery, walnuts and remaining mayonnaise to diced apples; toss until combined.
3. Line a serving bowl with lettuce leaves; spoon salad into center. Garnish with reserved apple slices. Makes 4 to 6 servings.

Cucumber & Strawberry Salad

1 small cucumber, peeled, thinly sliced
12 large strawberries, thinly sliced
Pinch of salt
Freshly ground white pepper to taste
2 tablespoons dry white wine

1. Arrange cucumber and strawberry slices in a shallow serving dish as shown in photo.
2. Sprinkle with salt and pepper. Drizzle with wine. Cover and refrigerate about 20 minutes before serving. Makes 4 servings.

Left to right: Cucumber & Strawberry Salad, Waldorf Salad

Curried Potato Salad

1-1/2 lbs. red potatoes, peeled
Salt to taste
6 tablespoons mayonnaise
1 teaspoon curry powder
1 tablespoon ketchup
1/4 cup plain yogurt
1 small onion, finely chopped
1 small green bell pepper, chopped

1. Cook potatoes in boiling salted water until tender. Drain well; cool slightly. Cut potatoes into cubes; place in a medium bowl.
2. In a small bowl, combine mayonnaise, curry powder, ketchup and yogurt. Pour mayonnaise mixture over potatoes. Add onion and bell pepper; toss until coated. Transfer to a serving dish. Makes 6 servings.

Red Salad

1 (8-oz.) head of red cabbage
5 tablespoons Garlic Dressing, page 25
1 head of radicchio
1 small red onion
1 bunch of radishes

1. Finely shred cabbage; place in a medium bowl. Add dressing; toss to combine. Cover and let stand 1 hour.
2. Separate radicchio into leaves, then tear into pieces. Thinly slice onion and radishes. Add radicchio pieces, onion slices and radish slices to bowl; toss to combine. Transfer to a salad bowl. Makes 6 to 8 servings.

Endive & Orange Salad

6 heads of Belgian endive
6 oranges
2 tablespoons chopped parsley
1/2 cup Honey & Lemon Dressing, page 25

1. Cut Belgian endive diagonally crosswise into 1/2-inch slices; place endive slices in a large salad bowl.
2. Remove peel and bitter, white pith from oranges. Section oranges, holding oranges over bowl so that any juice is included.
3. Add parsley and dressing; toss until combined. Makes 10 to 12 servings.

Spiced Rice Salad

3/4 cup dried apricots (3 oz.), chopped
2/3 cup long-grain rice
Salt to taste
1-1/3 cups water
1 tablespoon vegetable oil
1/2 cup sliced almonds
1 teaspoon freshly grated nutmeg
3 celery stalks, diced
4 green onions, sliced
1 tablespoon chopped cilantro
1/4 cup French dressing, page 25

1. Cover apricots with boiling water; let soak 1 hour. Drain well.
2. Combine rice, salt and water in a medium saucepan. Bring to a boil. Reduce heat, cover and simmer 15 minutes or until water is absorbed and rice is tender. Cool slightly.
3. Heat oil in a small skillet. Add almonds; sauté until golden, stirring. Add nutmeg; cook a few seconds.
4. Place warm rice and drained apricots in a salad bowl. Add spiced almonds and oil. Mix in celery, green onions and cilantro. Pour dressing over salad; toss thoroughly before serving. Makes 4 servings.

Variation
Substitute pitted, chopped dates for dried apricots. Omit soaking.

California Coleslaw

1/4 cup Honey & Lemon Dressing, page 25
1 Golden Delicious apple
2 oranges
1-1/3 cups white seedless grapes, halved
1 (8-oz.) head of white cabbage, finely shredded
2 tablespoons chopped chives
2 tablespoons roasted sunflower kernels

1. Pour dressing into a medium bowl. Core apple; thinly slice apple into dressing. Toss until thoroughly coated.
2. Remove peel and bitter, white pith from oranges. Section oranges; add orange sections to bowl. Add remaining ingredients; toss to combine. Transfer to a salad bowl. Makes 6 to 8 servings.

Clockwise from top: California Coleslaw, Red Salad, Curried Potato Salad

Chinese Salad

1 (1-inch) piece gingerroot, finely chopped
1/4 cup French Dressing, page 25
1 head of Chinese or napa cabbage
1/2 cucumber
4 oz. bean sprouts
6 green onions, chopped

To garnish:
1 tablespoon chopped parsley

1. In a small bowl, combine gingerroot and dressing; let stand 30 minutes.
2. Shred cabbage; cut cucumber into julienne strips. Combine shredded cabbage, cucumber strips, bean sprouts and green onions in a medium bowl.
3. Add dressing; toss until combined. Sprinkle with parsley. Makes 6 servings.

Sunchokes & Tomatoes

2 lbs. sunchokes (Jerusalem artichokes)
Salt to taste
3 tablespoons olive oil
4 tomatoes, peeled, chopped
1 teaspoon chopped fresh marjoram or 1/2 teaspoon
    dried leaf marjoram
Freshly ground pepper to taste

1. In a large saucepan, cook sunchokes in boiling salted water 20 minutes or until almost tender. Drain and cut into equal pieces.
2. Heat olive oil in a medium saucepan. Add tomatoes, marjoram and sunchokes. Season with salt and pepper. Cover and simmer 5 to 10 minutes or until sunchokes are tender.
3. Transfer to a warm serving dish. Serve immediately. Makes 4 servings.

Gazpacho Salad

1 each green, red and yellow bell pepper
4 large tomatoes
1 small cucumber, peeled
1 medium onion
1/4 cup chopped parsley

Garlic Dressing:
1/4 cup olive oil
2 tablespoons white-wine vinegar
2 garlic cloves, crushed
Pinch of ground cumin
1 teaspoon honey
2 green onions, chopped
Salt to taste
Freshly ground pepper to taste

To garnish:
Few ripe olives

1. Remove core and seeds from peppers; thinly slice peppers. Coarsely chop tomatoes. Remove seeds from cucumber; coarsely chop. Finely chop onion.
2. Layer peppers, tomatoes, cucumber and onion in a glass bowl. Sprinkle parsley over each layer.
3. In a small bowl, whisk all dressing ingredients until combined; pour over salad. Cover and let stand 15 minutes before serving. Top with olives. Makes 4 servings.

Red-Cabbage & Apple Salad

1 (12-oz.) head of red cabbage
1 small leek, sliced
6 tablespoons Vinaigrette Dressing, page 25
3 Red Delicious apples

1. Finely shred cabbage. Place shredded cabbage and leek in a salad bowl.
2. Add dressing; toss until combined. Marinate 1 hour, tossing occasionally.
3. Quarter, core and thinly slice apples. Add sliced apples to the bowl; toss again and serve. Makes 8 servings.

Tomato & Basil Salad

1 lb. tomatoes
Salt to taste
Freshly ground pepper to taste
3 tablespoons olive oil
2 tablespoons chopped fresh basil or 2 teaspoons
  dried leaf basil

The piquant flavor of basil enhances the flavor of tomatoes, and the mellowness of the olive oil brings out the full flavor of this delicious salad. Serve as a refreshing summer starter.

1. Thinly slice tomatoes. Arrange in layers in a shallow serving dish; sprinkle each layer with salt and pepper.
2. Pour oil over tomatoes; sprinkle with basil. Makes 4 servings.

Cucumber with Mint

1 large cucumber, thinly sliced
Salt to taste
1/3 cup packed mint, finely chopped
1/2 cup Yogurt Dressing, page 25

This refreshing salad is delicious to serve with curries or other spicy foods.

1. Place cucumber in a colander; sprinkle with salt. Let stand 30 minutes.
2. Rinse cucumber; dry with paper towels. Place in a shallow serving dish.
3. In a small bowl, combine mint and dressing. Pour over cucumber. Makes 4 to 6 servings.

Tomato & Leek Salad

1 lb. tomatoes, sliced
2 medium leeks, thinly sliced
1/4 cup Honey & Lemon Dressing, page 25
1 tablespoon chopped parsley

1. Arrange tomatoes and leeks in layers in a shallow serving dish, ending with leeks.
2. Pour dressing over top; sprinkle with parsley. Makes 4 servings.

Variation
Marinate leeks in dressing 15 minutes before combining with tomatoes for a more mellow flavor.

Top to bottom: Tomato & Basil Salad, Cucumber with Mint, Tomato & Leek Salad

Bell-Pepper & Salami Salad

Bell-Pepper & Salami Salad

4 each large green, red and yellow bell peppers
12 tomatoes
8 hard-cooked eggs
4 oz. ham slices
4 oz. salami slices
4 (2-oz.) cans anchovy fillets, drained
Ripe olives

Garlic & Herb Dressing:
4 garlic cloves, crushed
2 tablespoons chopped parsley and chives
2 tablespoons chopped chives
2 teaspoons dried leaf tarragon
2 teaspoons dried leaf chervil
2 teaspoons coarse-ground mustard
2 teaspoons honey
6 tablespoons lemon juice
3/4 cup olive oil
Salt to taste
Freshly ground pepper to taste

1. Position oven rack 4 to 6 inches from heat source. Preheat broiler.
2. Place whole peppers on a baking sheet. Broil until skins are charred. Cool; peel away skin. Remove and discard cores and seeds. Cut peppers into 1/2-inch strips.
3. Thickly slice tomatoes and eggs. Divide between 2 large salad bowls. Cut ham and salami into narrow strips; arrange over tomatoes and eggs. Place peppers around edges. Arrange anchovy fillets in a lattice pattern over salads; place olives on top.
4. Whisk dressing ingredients together in a medium bowl. Spoon 1/2 of dressing over each salad. Cover and refrigerate 20 minutes before serving. Makes 10 servings.

Spinach-Noodle Salad

8 oz. spinach noodles
Salt to taste
1/2 cup Vinaigrette Dressing, opposite
4 oz. mushrooms, thinly sliced
1 small garlic clove, if desired, crushed
4 oz. cooked ham, thinly sliced
1/3 cup grated Parmesan cheese (1 oz.)

1. Cook noodles in a large pan of boiling salted water according to package directions until tender. Do not overcook. Drain cooked noodles.
2. In a large bowl, combine dressing, mushrooms and garlic, if desired.
3. Add warm noodles; toss until coated with dressing.
4. Cut ham into strips the same width as noodles; add to salad. Toss to combine. Serve immediately, or cover and refrigerate up to 24 hours. Bring to room temperature before serving.
5. To serve, spoon into a serving bowl; sprinkle with Parmesan cheese. Makes 6 to 8 starters.

Salad Dressings

A well made salad dressing can transform a good salad into something really exciting. But it is most important to use good ingredients; the choice of oil is especially important. Oils are produced from various nuts, seeds and beans, and each has its own particular flavor. Unrefined oils have a superior flavor, especially olive oil, and are more expensive than refined oils. Always choose wine, cider or herb-flavored vinegars—malt vinegar is far too harsh.

Vinaigrette Dressing

3/4 cup olive oil
1/4 cup cider vinegar
1 teaspoon honey
1 garlic clove, crushed
2 tablespoons chopped mixed fresh herbs, such as
   mint, parsley, chives and thyme
Salt to taste
Freshly ground pepper to taste

1. Combine olive oil, vinegar, honey, garlic and herbs in a container with a tight-fitting lid. Season with salt and pepper.
2. Cover tightly; shake until blended before serving. Makes 1 cup.

Variation
Lemon or Lime Vinaigrette: Substitute 1/4 cup fresh lemon or lime juice for cider vinegar.

French Dressing

3/4 cup olive oil
1/4 cup white-wine vinegar
1 teaspoon Dijon-style mustard
1 garlic clove, crushed
1 teaspoon honey
Salt to taste
Freshly ground pepper to taste

1. Combine olive oil, vinegar, mustard, garlic and honey in a container with a tight-fitting lid. Season with salt and pepper.
2. Cover tightly; shake until blended before serving. Makes 1 cup.

Variations
Mustard Dressing: Add 2 tablespoons coarse-ground mustard; shake until combined.
Garlic Dressing: Add 4 crushed garlic cloves to dressing.

Honey & Lemon Dressing

1/4 cup lemon juice
2 tablespoons honey
3 tablespoons olive oil
Salt to taste
Freshly ground pepper to taste

1. Combine lemon juice, honey and olive oil in a small container with a tight-fitting lid. Season with salt and pepper.
2. Cover tightly; shake until blended before serving. Makes 1/2 cup.

Yogurt Dressing

1 (6-oz.) carton plain yogurt
1 garlic clove, crushed
1 tablespoon cider vinegar
1 teaspoon honey
Salt to taste
Freshly ground white pepper to taste

1. Combine yogurt, garlic, vinegar and honey in a small bowl.
2. Season with salt and pepper. Makes about 1/2 cup.

Variation
Herb Dressing: Place all ingredients in a blender or food processor fitted with the steel blade. Add 1/2 cup parsley, 1/4 cup chopped mint and 1/4 cup chopped chives. Blend until pureed. Cover and refrigerate until needed. Makes 1 cup.

Left to right: Watercress Soup, Cucumber Soup

Watercress Soup

2 bunches watercress
2 tablespoons butter or margarine
1 large onion, chopped
1 large Russet potato, peeled, diced
2 cups chicken stock
1 cup milk
Salt to taste
Freshly ground pepper to taste

---

1. Wash watercress thoroughly, removing any coarse stalks; drain. Melt butter or margarine in a large saucepan over medium heat. Add onion and potato; cook about 5 minutes or until they start to soften.
2. Stir in 1/2 of watercress, stock and milk. Season with salt and pepper; bring to a boil. Reduce heat. Cover and simmer 20 minutes. Cool slightly.
3. Process soup in a blender or food processor fitted with the steel blade; return to pan. Finely chop remaining watercress; stir chopped watercress into soup. Serve hot. Makes 4 servings.

Cucumber Soup

1 large cucumber, peeled
1 large garlic clove, crushed
2 tablespoons white-wine vinegar
1/2 cup packed mint leaves, chopped
1/2 pint dairy sour cream (1 cup)
1 teaspoon superfine sugar
Salt to taste
Freshly ground white pepper to taste
To finish:
About 1 cup milk or half and half
Mint sprigs

Accompany this refreshing cold soup with Melba toast.

1. Finely grate cucumber into a medium bowl. Stir in garlic, vinegar, mint, sour cream, sugar, salt and pepper.
2. Cover and refrigerate soup at least 2 hours or up to 8 hours before serving. Stir in milk or half and half to desired consistency.
3. Serve soup in chilled bowls and garnish each portion with a small mint sprig. Makes 4 to 6 servings.

Cream of Mussel Soup

To garnish:
Chopped chervil or parsley

2 lbs. mussels in shells, scrubbed, cleaned
1/2 cup dry white wine
1/2 cup water
1 onion, finely chopped
1 celery stalk, finely chopped
Bouquet Garni, page 30
1 whole clove
6 black peppercorns
2 tablespoons all-purpose flour creamed with 2
   tablespoons soft butter or margarine
1 cup milk
1 cup half and half
Salt to taste
Pinch of red (cayenne) pepper
Pinch of ground nutmeg

1. Combine mussels, wine, water, onion, celery, bouquet garni, clove and peppercorns in a large pan. Cover and cook over low heat until mussels open, about 4 to 6 minutes, shaking pan once or twice.
2. Discard any mussels that do not open. Remove mussels with a slotted spoon; set aside. Strain liquid into a bowl; let stand 5 minutes. Strain again through double cheesecloth into a medium saucepan. This is to remove any traces of sand. Discard vegetables and spices.
3. Stir in flour mixture. Stir in milk; cook until thickened, stirring constantly. Stir in half and half. Season with salt, red pepper and nutmeg. Remove from heat.
4. Remove mussels from shells; add to soup. Heat through; do not boil. Spoon into soup bowls; garnish with chervil or parsley. Makes 4 servings.

Cream of Mussel Soup

Lobster Bisque

Lobster Bisque

1 (1-lb.) lobster, cooked
3 tablespoons butter or margarine
1 medium onion, sliced
1 small carrot, sliced
1 celery stalk, sliced
1/4 cup all-purpose flour
2 cups milk
Red (cayenne) pepper to taste
Salt to taste
Freshly ground white pepper to taste
2 egg yolks
1/2 cup whipping cream
2 tablespoons dry sherry
2 tablespoons brandy, if desired

To garnish:
4 teaspoons caviar, if desired

1. Preheat oven to 350F (175C).
2. Remove all meat from lobster shell; dice and reserve meat. Place shell in a baking pan. Bake in preheated oven 20 minutes to dry out.
3. Pound baked shell as finely as possible. Melt butter or margarine in a medium saucepan over low heat. Add shell, onion, carrot and celery. Cover and cook 20 minutes, stirring occasionally.
4. Stir in flour; cook 2 minutes, stirring constantly. Gradually stir in milk, a little red pepper, salt and white pepper. Simmer 20 minutes, stirring occasionally.
5. Strain sauce through double cheesecloth, then return it to the pan. Discard any shell and the vegetables. In a small bowl, beat egg yolks and cream; stir in about 1/4 cup hot mixture. Return mixture to pan. Heat, stirring, until slightly thickened; do not boil. Add lobster meat, sherry and brandy, if desired.
6. Spoon into soup bowls; garnish each serving with 1 teaspoon caviar, if desired. Makes 4 servings.

Cream of Cauliflower Soup

3 tablespoons butter or margarine
1 medium onion, finely chopped
1 (1-lb.) cauliflower, divided into flowerets
2 cups chicken stock
Salt to taste
Freshly ground pepper to taste
2 teaspoons chopped fresh chervil or 1 teaspoon dried
    chervil
2 cups milk

To garnish:
Chervil sprigs, if desired

This is a simple version of a classic French soup. Recipe can be doubled.

1. Melt 2 tablespoons butter or margarine in a medium saucepan over medium heat. Add onion; sauté until soft, about 5 minutes.
2. Add cauliflowerets, reserving a few for garnish. Reduce heat. Cook cauliflower about 5 minutes or until coated in butter and onion, stirring constantly.
3. Increase heat. Stir in stock; bring to a boil. Reduce heat. Add salt, pepper and 1/2 of chervil. Half cover with a lid. Simmer 15 minutes or until cauliflower is tender, stirring occasionally. Cool slightly.
4. Process in a blender or food processor fitted with the steel blade until pureed. Return puree to the pan; stir in milk. Bring almost to boiling, stirring constantly. Reduce heat and simmer about 5 minutes. Check consistency of soup, stirring in a little extra milk if it seems too thick.
5. Meanwhile, melt remaining 1 tablespoon butter or margarine in a small saucepan. Add reserved cauliflowerets; toss gently in butter or margarine 1 to 2 minutes.
6. Pour soup into a warmed tureen or 4 individual bowls. Top with cauliflowerets, then sprinkle with remaining chervil. Serve hot. Makes 4 servings.

Summer Vegetable Soup

8 large ripe tomatoes
2 garlic cloves
1/2 small onion
1/2 cucumber
1 green bell pepper
1 red bell pepper
1 thyme sprig or 1 teaspoon dried leaf thyme
1 basil sprig or 1 teaspoon dried leaf basil
2 parsley sprigs
6 tablespoons olive oil
1/4 cup lemon juice
2 cups tomato juice, chilled
Few drops hot-pepper sauce

To serve:
Garlic-flavored croutons
Ripe olives
Capers

1. Coarsely chop tomatoes, garlic, onion, cucumber and bell peppers.
2. Place all chopped ingredients in a blender or food processor fitted with the steel blade; process until smooth. Add thyme, basil and parsley; process until combined.
3. Pour into a bowl; cover and refrigerate until chilled. Just before serving, combine olive oil and lemon juice in a medium bowl. Add tomato juice and hot-pepper sauce; gradually stir into soup.
4. Garnish with croutons; serve olives and capers as accompaniments. Makes 6 servings.

Bouquet Garni

To make a bouquet garni, cut a 3-inch cheesecloth square. Place 2 bay leaves, 2 or 3 sprigs each of parsley and thyme or marjoram, 6 peppercorns and 1 garlic clove, if desired, on cheesecloth. Bring edge of cheesecloth up to form a bag. Tie securely with kitchen string.

Creamy Zucchini & Brie Soup

2 medium zucchini, sliced
3 small Russet potatoes, peeled, quartered
1 tablespoon olive oil
Salt to taste
4 oz. ripe Brie cheese, rind removed, diced
Freshly ground white pepper to taste
1/4 cup whipping cream

Serve with crisp French bread. Recipe can be doubled.

1. Combine zucchini, potatoes, oil and 1 teaspoon salt in a large saucepan. Cover with water. Bring to a boil. Reduce heat; simmer 15 to 20 minutes or until potatoes are tender. Cool slightly.
2. Remove zucchini and potatoes with a slotted spoon. Process in a blender or food processor until pureed. Pour cooking liquid into a medium bowl. Add Brie and 1 cup cooking liquid to blender or food processor. Process until smooth.
3. Return mixture to the pan; add 1/2 cup cooking liquid from vegetables. Bring almost to boiling, stirring constantly. Season with salt and pepper.
4. Check consistency of soup; add more vegetable liquid or water if it is too thick. Pour into 4 individual bowls; swirl a spoonful of cream into each. Serve hot. Makes 4 servings.

Left to right: Stuffed Smoked-Salmon Rolls, page 12; Cream of Cauliflower Soup; Creamy Zucchini & Brie Soup

Quick Gazpacho

1/4 cup lemon juice
4 teaspoons white-wine vinegar
1 teaspoon Worcestershire sauce
4 cups tomato juice (1 qt.)
2 to 3 garlic cloves, crushed
6 large tomatoes, peeled, finely chopped
1 (4-inch) cucumber piece, grated or chopped
2 to 3 tablespoons finely grated onion
1 green bell pepper, finely chopped
Salt to taste
Freshly ground black pepper to taste

To serve:
Chopped fresh herbs
1 cucumber, chopped
1 green bell pepper, chopped
2 tomatoes, chopped

1. Combine lemon juice, vinegar, Worcestershire sauce, tomato juice and garlic in a medium bowl. Stir in tomatoes, cucumber, onion and bell pepper.
2. If a smooth soup if preferred, pour into a blender or food processor fitted with the steel blade; process until pureed. For a chunky soup, do not process. Season with salt and pepper.
3. Pour into a bowl. Cover tightly; refrigerate until chilled or up to 24 hours. To serve, spoon into individual bowls; sprinkle with chopped herbs. Serve chopped vegetables separately to sprinkle over soup. Makes 8 servings.

Left to right: Quick Gazpacho, Curry Soup

Curry Soup

2 tablespoons butter or margarine
1 large onion, chopped
1 large carrot, chopped
1 garlic clove, crushed
1 tablespoon all-purpose flour
1 to 1-1/2 teaspoons curry powder
1-1/2 cups chicken stock
2 teaspoons lemon juice
Salt to taste
Freshly ground pepper to taste
Dash of hot-pepper sauce
1 bay leaf
1/2 cup half and half

To garnish:
4 cooked shrimp or croutons
Chopped parsley

1. Melt butter or margarine in a medium saucepan. Add onion, carrot and garlic; sauté until wilted. Stir in flour and curry powder to taste; cook 2 minutes, stirring.
2. Gradually stir in stock. Bring to a boil. Add lemon juice, salt, pepper, hot-pepper sauce and bay leaf. Reduce heat. Cover and simmer about 20 minutes or until vegetables are soft. Discard bay leaf; cool soup slightly.
3. Process in a blender or food processor fitted with the steel blade until pureed. Pour into a bowl; cover and refrigerate until chilled. Stir in half and half; taste for seasoning.
4. Pour into individual bowls; sprinkle with parsley; top with shrimp or croutons. Makes 4 servings.

Variation
To serve soup hot, reheat after pureeing. Add half and half; heat through.

Shrimp Bisque

2 tablespoons butter or margarine
1 onion, finely chopped
1 garlic clove, crushed
1/4 cup all-purpose flour
1 (15-oz.) can tomatoes and 1 (8-oz.) can tomatoes
Juice of 1/2 lemon
1 Bouquet Garni, page 7
Salt to taste
Freshly ground pepper to taste
2 tablespoons dry white wine
8 oz. cod or haddock fillets, cut in 1-inch pieces
8 oz. peeled shrimp, coarsely chopped

1. Melt butter or margarine in a large saucepan. Add onion and garlic; cook 5 minutes, stirring occasionally. Stir in flour; cook 2 minutes, stirring constantly.
2. Gradually stir in tomatoes with their juice and lemon juice. Add bouquet garni. Season with salt and pepper. Bring to a boil. Reduce heat. Cover and simmer 25 minutes. Remove bouquet garni. Cool slightly.
3. Process tomato mixture in a blender or food processor fitted with the steel blade until smooth. Return to the pan; stir in wine, fish and shrimp. Cook 5 to 10 minutes or until fish turns from transparent to opaque. Spoon into individual soup bowls. Makes 6 servings.

Clockwise from left: Shrimp Bisque, Avocado Soup, Almond Soup

Avocado Soup

2 ripe avocados
Juice of 1/2 lemon
2 (14-1/2-oz.) cans condensed chicken broth
3/4 cup whipping cream
Pinch of red (cayenne) pepper
2 drops hot-pepper sauce
Salt to taste
Freshly ground white pepper to taste

To garnish:
Thin lemon wedges
Parsley sprigs

1. Cut avocados in half lengthwise, remove pits and scoop out all flesh. Combine avocados and lemon juice in a blender or food processor fitted with the steel blade; process until smooth.
2. Transfer to a bowl; stir in remaining ingredients. Cover and refrigerate several hours before serving. Spoon into individual bowls. Garnish with lemon wedges and parsley sprigs. Makes 4 to 6 servings.

Almond Soup

2 tablespoons butter or margarine
1 small onion, finely chopped
3 tablespoons all-purpose flour
1-1/2 cups chicken stock
6 oz. sliced almonds
1 bay leaf
Salt to taste
3/4 cup whipping cream

To garnish:
Toasted sliced almonds

1. Melt butter or margarine in a medium saucepan. Add onion; cook 5 minutes or until soft. Stir in flour; cook 2 minutes, stirring constantly.
2. Gradually stir in stock. Add almonds, bay leaf and salt. Bring to a boil. Reduce heat. Cover and simmer 20 minutes. Cool slightly; remove bay leaf.
3. Process in a blender or food processor fitted with the steel blade until smooth. Transfer to a bowl; cover and refrigerate at least 2 hours or up to 8 hours.
4. Just before serving, stir in cream. Spoon into individual bowls; top with toasted almonds. Makes 4 to 6 servings.

Mussel Chowder

2 lbs. mussels in shells, scrubbed, cleaned
8 oz. white fish fillets, skinned
3 tablespoons butter or margarine
1 onion, chopped
2 celery stalks, chopped
1 garlic clove, crushed
3 tablespoons all-purpose flour
1-1/2 cups fish stock
1/2 cup dry white wine
Salt to taste
Freshly ground white pepper to taste
1 Bouquet Garni, page 30
1 cup cooked long-grain rice
1/2 teaspoon crumbled saffron threads
2 egg yolks
3 tablespoons half and half
2 tablespoons chopped parsley

1. Discard any mussels that do not close when given a sharp tap. Cut fish into 1-1/2-inch pieces.
2. Melt butter or margarine in a large saucepan. Add onion, celery and garlic; cook 2 minutes, stirring occasionally. Stir in flour; cook 2 minutes, stirring constantly.
3. Gradually stir in stock; bring to a boil. Stir in wine; season with salt and pepper. Add fish, bouquet garni and mussels. Cover and cook 5 to 7 minutes or until fish turns from transparent to opaque and mussel shells have opened. Discard any mussels that do not open.
4. Stir in rice and saffron; heat through. Discard bouquet garni. In a small bowl, blend egg yolks and half and half. Pour 1 tablespoon hot soup into egg mixture; mix well. Return warmed mixture to remaining soup; stir in parsley. Heat through; do not boil. Makes 6 servings.

Seafood & Saffron Soup

2 large onions, chopped
2 medium Russet potatoes, diced
2 cups milk
1 cup fish stock or chicken stock
1-1/2 lbs. skinned white fish fillets, cut in 1-1/2-inch pieces
1/2 cup white wine
3/4 teaspoon crumbled saffron threads
Salt to taste
Freshly ground pepper to taste
4 oz. peeled cooked shrimp
4 sea scallops, coarsely chopped
3/4 cup whipping cream

To garnish:
4 to 6 cooked shrimp

1. Combine onions, potatoes, milk and stock in a large saucepan. Bring to a boil. Reduce heat. Cover and simmer 15 minutes or until potatoes are soft. Cool slighty.
2. Process potato mixture in a blender or food processor fitted with the steel blade until smooth. Return soup to the pan; add fish and scallops. Simmer 5 to 10 minutes or until fish turns from transparent to opaque.
3. Stir in wine and saffron; season with salt and pepper. Stir in shrimp, scallops and cream. Heat through; do not boil. Garnish with shrimp; serve immediately. Makes 4 to 6 servings.

Left to right: Seafood & Saffron Soup, Mussel Chowder

APPETIZERS FOR BUFFETS

Turkey Loaf

1-1/2 lbs. cooked turkey meat, finely minced
1 lb. lean ground beef
1 onion, minced
8 bacon slices, minced
1 garlic clove, minced
1 tablespoon tomato paste
1 tablespoon dried leaf tarragon
Salt to taste
Freshly ground pepper to taste
About 1/2 cup turkey stock or chicken stock
2 bay leaves

1. Grease an 8" x 4" terrine dish or loaf pan. Preheat oven to 350F (175C).
2. In a medium bowl, combine all ingredients, except bay leaves, with enough stock to moisten. Turn into greased dish or pan; arrange bay leaves on top. Cover with foil.
3. Bake in preheated oven 2 hours or until juices are clear when center is pierced with a skewer. Cool slightly; remove foil. Place a long dish on top of terrine; add a 1-pound weight to dish. Refrigerate until chilled. Discard bay leaves. Cut into thin slices. Makes about 12 servings.

Variation
Turkey Galantine: Make turkey mixture as above. Roll in a floured cloth; tie ends. Poach in simmering water 2-1/2 hours. Cool under a weighted plate as above. Remove cloth; cut into thin slices.

Turkey Mousse

2 (1/4-oz.) envelopes gelatin (5 teaspoons)
2 cups turkey stock or chicken stock
8 oz. cooked turkey breast, finely diced
1 tablespoon tomato paste
1 teaspoon dried leaf tarragon
2 egg yolks
1/2 pint whipping cream (1 cup)
5 tablespoons brandy
Salt to taste
Freshly ground pepper to taste

To serve:
Butter lettuce leaves
1 head of Belgian endive, separated into leaves
Orange wedges

1. Grease a 1-quart ring mold. In a small saucepan, combine gelatin and 1/2 cup stock. Stir well; let stand 3 minutes. Stir over low heat until gelatin dissolves; cool slightly.
2. Combine remaining stock, gelatin mixture and remaining ingredients, except lettuce, endive and oranges, in a blender or food processor fitted with the steel blade. Process until smooth. Pour into greased mold. Cover and refrigerate until set.
3. Run tip of a knife around edge of mold to loosen. Place a serving plate over mousse; invert. Rinse a towel under hot running water; wring dry. Wrap hot towel around outside of mold. Let stand 10 to 15 seconds. Carefully unmold mousse onto plate.
4. Fill center of mousse with lettuce leaves. Garnish edge of plate with Belgian endive and orange wedges. Makes about 10 servings.

Top to bottom: Turkey Loaf, Turkey Mousse

Country-Style Chicken Pâté

1 (3-lb.) broiler-fryer chicken
4 oz. chicken livers, chopped
8 oz. bacon slices, minced
1 tablespoon dried leaf tarragon
1 onion, finely chopped
2 garlic cloves, crushed
1 tablespoon tomato paste
1/2 cup dry red wine
Salt to taste
Freshly ground pepper to taste
1 teaspoon dried leaf thyme
2 bay leaves

To garnish:
Lettuce leaves
Tomato slices

1. Preheat oven to 325F (165C). Grease a 9" x 5" loaf pan.
2. Remove and discard skin and bones from chicken meat. Finely chop meat. In a medium bowl, combine chopped chicken, livers, bacon, tarragon, onion, garlic, tomato paste, wine, salt and pepper. Spoon into greased loaf pan; arrange bay leaves on top. Cover with foil.
3. Bake in preheated oven 2-1/2 hours or until juices are clear when center is pierced with a skewer. Cool slightly. Cover and refrigerate until chilled.
4. To serve, cut into thin slices; garnish with lettuce and tomato. Makes about 12 servings.

Chicken Mousse

2 (1/4-oz.) envelopes gelatin (5 teaspoons)
2 cups chicken stock
1 lb. cooked chicken meat, shredded
5 tablespoons dry sherry
1 teaspoon dried leaf tarragon
Freshly ground pepper to taste
1/2 pint whipping cream (1 cup)
2 teaspoons tomato paste

To garnish:
Watercress

1. Lightly grease a 5- to 6-cup mold. In a small saucepan, combine gelatin and 1/2 cup stock. Stir well; let stand 3 minutes. Stir over low heat until gelatin dissolves; cool slightly.
2. Combine remaining stock, gelatin mixture and remaining ingredients in a blender or food processor fitted with the steel blade. Process until smooth. Pour into greased mold. Cover and refrigerate until set.
3. Run tip of a knife around edge of mold to loosen. Place a serving plate over mousse; invert. Rinse a towel under hot running water; wring dry. Wrap hot towel around outside of mold. Let stand 10 to 15 seconds. Carefully unmold mousse onto plate.
4. Garnish with watercress. Makes 6 to 8 servings.

Ardennes Pâté

2 lbs. pork, diced
1 lb. ground veal
1-1/2 lbs. chicken livers, chopped
1/2 cup brandy
2 teaspoons dried leaf thyme
2 tablespoons green peppercorns, drained
Salt to taste
Freshly ground pepper to taste
8 to 12 bacon slices

To garnish:
Thyme sprigs
Lemon slices

To serve:
Toast

1. Combine pork, veal and chicken livers in a large bowl. Stir in brandy, thyme, peppercorns, salt and pepper. Cover and refrigerate 2 hours.
2. Lightly grease a 9" x 5" loaf pan. Preheat oven to 350F (175C).
3. Spoon mixture into greased loaf pan. Cover top of pâté with bacon. Cover with foil; place in a roasting pan. Pour in enough boiling water to come halfway up the sides of loaf pan.
4. Cook in preheated oven 1-1/2 hours or until juices are clear when center is pierced with a skewer.
5. Cool slightly. Cover and refrigerate until chilled. Turn out of pan. Cut into thin slices to serve. Garnish with thyme and lemon slices; serve with toast. Makes about 16 servings.

Herbed Chicken Loaf

1 (3-lb.) broiler-fryer chicken
4 bacon slices, minced
8 oz. lean ground beef
1 onion, minced
1 teaspoon dried mixed herbs, such as tarragon, thyme and oregano
2 garlic cloves, crushed
5 tablespoons dry white wine
Salt to taste
Freshly ground pepper to taste
2 bay leaves

1. Preheat oven to 325F (165C). Grease a 9" x 5" loaf pan.
2. Remove and discard skin and bones from chicken meat. Finely chop meat. In a medium bowl, combine chopped chicken, bacon, beef, onion, herbs, garlic, wine, salt and pepper. Spoon into greased loaf pan; arrange bay leaves on top. Cover with foil.
3. Bake in preheated oven 2-1/2 hours or until juices are clear when center is pierced with a skewer. Cool slightly. Cover and refrigerate until chilled. Discard bay leaves.
4. Cut in thin slices to serve. Makes about 12 servings.

Clockwise from top left: Country-Style Chicken Pâté, Herbed Chicken Loaf, Chicken Mousse

Top to bottom: Fresh Salmon Mousse, Smoked-Salmon Mousse

Smoked-Salmon Mousse

1/2 cup butter or margarine, melted
2-1/4 cups fine cracker crumbs
3 tablespoons chopped parsley
Salt to taste
Freshly ground pepper to taste

Filling:
2 (8-oz.) pkgs. cream cheese, room temperature
Grated peel and juice of 1/2 lemon
4 eggs, separated
1 tablespoon tomato paste
1/2 pint dairy sour cream (1 cup)
Salt to taste
Freshly ground white pepper to taste
1 (1/4-oz.) envelope gelatin (about 1 tablespoon)
1/4 cup water
3/4 cup chopped pimento-stuffed olives
6 oz. smoked-salmon trimmings, minced

Topping:
2 (3-oz.) pkgs. cream cheese, room temperature
3 tablespoons mayonnaise
8 pimento-stuffed olives, sliced
1/4 cup chopped parsley

1. Grease a 10- to 12-inch springform pan. To make crumb mixture, in a large bowl, combine butter or margarine, cracker crumbs, parsley, salt and pepper. Press evenly over the bottom of greased pan. Refrigerate until chilled.
2. To make filling, place cheese in a large bowl. Beat in lemon peel, lemon juice, egg yolks, tomato paste, sour cream, salt and pepper; set aside.
3. In a small saucepan, combine gelatin and water. Stir well; let stand 3 minutes. Stir over low heat until gelatin dissolves; cool slightly. Beat cooled gelatin into cheese mixture. Let stand until mixture mounds when dropped from a spoon.
4. Beat egg whites until stiff but not dry; fold beaten egg whites, olives and salmon into cheese mixture. Spoon mixture into prepared pan; smooth top. Cover and refrigerate 3 to 4 hours or until filling is set.
5. Run tip of a knife around edge of pan to loosen. Ease side of pan carefully away from mousse. With mousse still on pan bottom, place on a serving plate.
6. To make topping, in a small bowl, beat cheese and mayonnaise until smooth. Spoon into a pastry bag fitted with a rosette tip. Pipe cheese mixture around edge of mousse. Garnish with sliced olives and parsley. Makes 10 to 12 servings.

Fresh Salmon Mousse

1/2 cup butter or margarine, melted
2-1/4 cups fine cracker crumbs
Grated peel of 1 lemon
Salt to taste
Freshly ground pepper to taste

Filling:
2 (8-oz.) pkgs. cream cheese, room temperature
Grated peel and juice of 1/2 lemon
4 eggs, separated
About 8 oz. cooked or canned salmon, flaked
1/2 medium cucumber, peeled, coarsely grated
1/2 pint whipping cream (1 cup)
1/4 cup mayonnaise
Salt to taste
Freshly ground white pepper to taste
4 teaspoons gelatin powder
1/4 cup water

Topping:
6 tablespoons mayonnaise
Thin lemon slices, halved
Cucumber slices
Paprika

1. Grease a 10- to 12-inch springform pan. To make crumb mixture, in a large bowl, combine butter or margarine, cracker crumbs, lemon peel, salt and pepper. Press evenly over the bottom of greased pan. Refrigerate until chilled.
2. To make filling, place cheese in a large bowl. Beat in lemon peel, lemon juice, egg yolks, salmon, cucumber, cream, mayonnaise, salt and pepper; set aside.
3. In a small saucepan, combine gelatin and water. Stir well; let stand 3 minutes. Stir over low heat until gelatin dissolves; cool slightly. Beat cooled gelatin into cheese mixture. Let stand until mixture mounds when dropped from a spoon.
4. Beat egg whites until stiff but not dry; fold beaten egg whites into cheese mixture. Spoon mixture into prepared pan; smooth top. Cover and refrigerate 3 to 4 hours or until filling is set.
5. Run tip of a knife around edge of pan to loosen. Ease side of pan carefully away from mousse. With mousse still on pan bottom, place on a serving plate.
6. Spread mayonnaise evenly over top of mousse. Garnish with lemon and cucumber slices and sprinkle with paprika, as shown in photo. Makes 10 to 12 servings.

Left to right: Summer Mousse, Layered Salad Mousse, Blue-Cheese Mousse

Summer Mousse

1/2 cup butter or margarine, melted
2-1/4 cups fine cracker crumbs
2 tablespoons chopped parsley
Salt to taste
Freshly ground pepper to taste

Filling:
2 (8-oz.) pkgs. cream cheese, room temperature
4 eggs, separated
1 garlic clove, crushed
Salt to taste
Freshly ground white pepper to taste
1/2 pint whipping cream (1 cup)
1 tablespoon chopped fresh tarragon or 1 teaspoon
    dried leaf tarragon
1 tablespoon chopped fresh basil or 1 teaspoon dried
    leaf basil
1 bunch of watercress, large stems removed
4 green onions, chopped
1 (1/4-oz.) envelope gelatin (about 1 tablespoon)
1/4 cup water
6 tablespoons chopped fresh parsley

Topping:
2 (3-oz.) pkgs. cream cheese, room temperature
3 tablespoons mayonnaise
Small watercress sprigs

1. Grease a 10- to 12-inch springform pan. To make crumb mixture, in a large bowl, combine butter or margarine, cracker crumbs, parsley, salt and pepper. Press evenly over the bottom of greased pan. Refrigerate until chilled.
2. To make filling, place cheese in a large bowl. Beat in egg yolks, garlic, salt and pepper; set aside. In a blender or food processor fitted with the steel blade, process cream, tarragon, basil and watercress until smooth. Beat herbed cream and green onions into the cheese mixture; set aside.
3. In a small saucepan, combine gelatin and water. Stir well; let stand 3 minutes. Stir over low heat until gelatin dissolves; cool slightly. Beat cooled gelatin into cheese mixture. Let stand until mixture mounds when dropped from a spoon.
4. Beat egg whites until stiff but not dry; fold beaten egg whites into cheese mixture. Spoon 1/2 of cheese mixture into prepared pan; smooth top. Sprinkle with parsley, then top with remaining cheese mixture and smooth the surface. Cover and refrigerate 3 to 4 hours or until filling is set.
5. Run tip of a knife around edge of pan to loosen. Ease side of pan carefully away from mousse. With mousse still on pan bottom, place on a serving plate.
6. To make topping, in a small bowl, beat cheese and mayonnaise until smooth. Spread cheese mixture on top of mousse. Garnish with watercress sprigs. Makes 10 to 12 servings.

Layered Salad Mousse

1/2 cup butter or margarine, melted
1-3/4 cups fine cracker crumbs
2/3 cup grated Parmesan cheese (2 oz.)
Salt to taste
Freshly ground pepper to taste

Filling:
2 (8-oz.) pkgs. cream cheese, room temperature
4 eggs, separated
1 cup grated Parmesan cheese (3 oz.)
1/2 cup whipping cream
1/2 cup mayonnaise
Salt to taste
Freshly ground white pepper to taste
1 (1/4-oz.) envelope gelatin (about 1 tablespoon)
1/2 cup water
1 large red bell pepper, cut into thin strips or finely
    chopped
1/3 large cucumber, thinly sliced
4 oz. sliced salami, cut into strips

To garnish:
1 (3-oz.) pkg. cream cheese, room temperature
1 tablespoon milk
6 salami slices
Onion slices, if desired, separated into rings

1. Grease a 10- to 12-inch springform pan. To make crumb mixture, in a large bowl, combine butter or margarine, cracker crumbs, cheese, salt and pepper. Press evenly over the bottom of greased pan. Refrigerate until chilled.
2. To make filling, place cheese in a large bowl. Beat in egg yolks, Parmesan cheese, cream, mayonnaise, salt and pepper; set aside.
3. In a small saucepan, combine gelatin and water. Stir well; let stand 3 minutes. Stir over low heat until gelatin dissolves; cool slightly. Beat cooled gelatin into cheese mixture. Let stand until mixture mounds when dropped from a spoon.
4. Beat egg whites until stiff but not dry; fold beaten egg whites into cheese mixture. Spoon 1/4 of cheese mixture into prepared pan; smooth top. Top with bell pepper. Add another 1/4 of cheese mixture; smooth top. Top with sliced cucumber. Add another 1/4 of cheese mixture; smooth top. Top with salami. Add remaining cheese mixture. Cover and refrigerate 3 to 4 hours or until filling is set.
5. Run tip of a knife around edge of pan to loosen. Ease side of pan carefully away from mousse. With mousse still on pan bottom, place on a serving plate.
6. To garnish, beat cheese and milk until smooth. Spoon into a pastry bag fitted with a rosette tip. Form salami slices into cones; pipe cream cheese into salami cones. Arrange salami cones around edge of mousse. Arrange onion slices in center of mousse, if desired. Makes 10 to 12 servings.

Blue-Cheese Mousse

1/2 cup butter or margarine, melted
2-1/4 cups fine cracker crumbs
2 tablespoons poppy seeds
Garlic salt to taste
Freshly ground pepper to taste

Filling:
1 (8-oz.) pkg. cream cheese, room temperature
1 (3-oz.) pkg. cream cheese, room temperature
6 oz. blue cheese, crumbled
4 eggs, separated
1 teaspoon Dijon-style mustard
1/2 pint whipping cream (1 cup)
Garlic salt to taste
Freshly ground white pepper to taste
1 (1/4-oz.) envelope gelatin (about 1 tablespoon)
1/4 cup water
4 oz. walnuts, chopped

To garnish:
Paprika
12 walnut halves
1 (3-oz.) pkg. cream cheese, room temperature
Small grape cluster

1. Grease a 10- to 12-inch springform pan. To make crumb mixture, in a large bowl, combine butter or margarine, cracker crumbs, poppy seeds, garlic salt and pepper. Press evenly over the bottom of greased pan. Refrigerate until chilled.
2. To make filling, place cheeses in a large bowl. Beat in egg yolks, mustard, cream, garlic salt and pepper; set aside.
3. In a small saucepan, combine gelatin and water. Stir well; let stand 3 minutes. Stir over low heat until gelatin dissolves; cool slightly. Beat cooled gelatin into cheese mixture. Let stand until mixture mounds when dropped from a spoon.
4. Beat egg whites until stiff but not dry; fold beaten egg whites and walnuts into cheese mixture. Spoon mixture into prepared pan; smooth top. Cover and refrigerate 3 to 4 hours or until filling is set.
5. Run tip of a knife around edge of pan to loosen. Ease side of pan carefully away from mousse. With mousse still on pan bottom, place on a serving plate.
6. To garnish, sprinkle top lightly with paprika. Sandwich walnut halves together with cheese. Arrange walnut-half sandwiches around edge of top. Place grape cluster in center. Makes 10 to 12 servings.

CANAPÉS & HORS D'OEUVRES

Canapés
For canapés, mound or pipe any of the following spreads on buttered, toasted bread or crackers. Top with the suggested garnishes.

Walnut-Cream Cheese Spread

1/2 (8-oz.) pkg. cream cheese, room temperature
1/4 cup walnuts, finely chopped
1/2 teaspoon red (cayenne) pepper
Salt to taste

To garnish:
About 1 cup walnut halves

1. In a small bowl, combine cream cheese, walnuts and red pepper. Season with salt. Cover and refrigerate up to 2 days, if desired. Bring to room temperature before serving.
2. Top each canapé with 1 walnut half. Makes about 1 cup.

Cucumber-Cream Cheese Spread

1/2 (8-oz.) pkg. cream cheese, room temperature
1/2 medium cucumber, peeled, seeded, finely chopped
Salt to taste

To garnish:
Chopped chives

1. In a small bowl, combine cream cheese and cucumber. Season with salt. Cover and refrigerate up to 2 days, if desired. Bring to room temperature before serving.
2. Top each canapé with chopped chives. Makes about 1 cup.

Bacon-Cream Cheese Spread

1/2 (8-oz.) pkg. cream cheese, room temperature
4 bacon slices, crisp-cooked, crumbled

To garnish:
1 green bell pepper, sliced

1. In a small bowl, combine cream cheese and bacon. Cover and refrigerate up to 2 days, if desired. Bring to room temperature before serving.
2. Top each canapé with 2 bell-pepper strips. Makes about 1 cup.

Pimento-Cream Cheese Spread

1/2 (8-oz.) cream cheese, room temperature
1/3 cup pimento-stuffed olives, finely chopped

To garnish:
About 6 pimento-stuffed olives, sliced

1. In a small bowl, mix cream cheese and chopped olives. Cover and refrigerate up to 2 days, if desired. Bring to room temperature before serving.
2. Top each canapé with 1 olive slice. Makes about 1 cup.

Tuna Spread

1 (6-oz.) can tuna, drained, flaked
1/4 cup dairy sour cream
Salt to taste
Freshly ground pepper to taste

To garnish:
3 sweet dill pickles, sliced crosswise

1. In a medium bowl, lightly combine tuna and sour cream. Season with salt and pepper. Cover and refrigerate up to 24 hours, if desired.
2. Top each canapé with a pickle slice. Makes about 1-1/4 cups.

Date-Cream Cheese Spread

1/2 (8-oz.) pkg. cream cheese, room temperature
1/3 cup pitted dates (about 2 oz.), finely chopped
Salt to taste

1. In a small bowl, combine cream cheese and dates. Season with salt. Cover and refrigerate up to 2 days, if desired. Bring to room temperature before serving.
2. Makes about 1-1/4 cups.

Top to bottom: Crackers with different spreads, Tuna Spread in bowl

Ham Rolls

Horseradish Cream:
1/2 cup whipping cream
2 tablespoons prepared horseradish
1 teaspoon white-wine vinegar
Salt to taste
Freshly ground white pepper to taste
Rolls:
1 lb. thinly sliced ham
1 lb. fresh asparagus or 1 (10-oz.) pkg. frozen
  asparagus, cooked

To garnish:
Lemon wedges

This is a luxurious dinner starter or it can be used as part of a buffet.

1. To make horseradish cream, whip cream until soft peaks form. Beat in horseradish, vinegar, salt and pepper to taste.
2. Cut ham into pieces about 3 inches square. Cut each asparagus spear in half crosswise. Lay ham pieces flat on a board; place 1 asparagus piece in the center of each ham piece.
3. Spoon a little horseradish cream over asparagus; roll up ham neatly. Arrange on a serving platter. Makes about 24 rolls.

Salmon Spread

1 (8-oz.) can red salmon, drained, flaked
1/4 cup mayonnaise
1 tablespoon lemon juice
Few drops of hot-pepper sauce
Buttered, toasted bread or crackers

To garnish:
Red (cayenne) pepper
Watercress sprigs

---

1. In a medium bowl, combine salmon, mayonnaise, lemon juice and hot-pepper sauce. Cover and refrigerate up to 24 hours, if desired.
2. To serve, spread on buttered toasted bread or crackers. Sprinkle with red pepper; garnish with watercress sprigs. Makes about 1-1/2 cups.

Chicken & Mushroom Vol-au-Vents

2 (17-1/4-oz.) pkgs. frozen puff pastry, thawed
2 eggs, beaten
Filling:
3 tablespoons butter or margarine
8 oz. mushrooms, finely chopped
5 tablespoons all-purpose flour
1-1/2 cups milk
1/2 cup whipping cream
1/2 teaspoon ground mace
Salt to taste
Freshly ground pepper to taste
12 oz. cooked chicken, finely diced

To garnish:
Parsley sprigs

---

1. Preheat oven to 400F (205C). Dampen 2 baking sheets with water.
2. Unfold 1 pastry sheet at a time on a lightly floured board. Roll out dough to 1/4 inch thick. Cut into circles with a 3-inch round fluted cutter. Place circles on dampened baking sheets; brush with beaten eggs. Mark centers of each circle with a 2-inch round cutter, without cutting through dough.
3. Bake in preheated oven 15 minutes or until puffed and golden brown.
4. Meanwhile, make filling. Melt butter or margarine in a medium saucepan over medium heat. Add mushrooms; sauté 2 minutes or until juices form. Stir in flour; cook 2 minutes, stirring constantly. Slowly stir in milk. Cook, stirring constantly, until thickened.
5. Let cool 1 to 2 minutes, then stir in whipping cream, mace, salt and pepper. Fold in chicken; cook over very low heat until heated through. Taste and adjust seasoning.
6. Remove pastry shells from oven; let cool slightly. Remove tops with a sharp knife and reserve. Scoop out any soft pastry with a teaspoon; spoon filling into each vol-au-vent and replace reserved tops.
7. Garnish each vol-au-vent with 1 small parsley sprig, transfer to a warm serving platter and serve immediately. Makes about 50 appetizers.

Clockwise from left: Chicken & Mushroom Vol-au-Vents, Ham Rolls, Salted Nuts, Stuffed Grapes, Stuffed Dates, Stuffed Prunes

Salted Nuts

6 tablespoons corn oil
6 tablespoons butter or margarine
1 lb. shelled mixed nuts, such as almonds, peanuts,
  cashews and walnuts
Salt to taste

1. Heat oil and butter or margarine in a skillet over medium heat. Add nuts; sauté 5 minutes, shaking pan, until browned on all sides.
2. Remove from pan with a slotted spoon; drain well on paper towels. Sprinkle with salt. Cool, then spoon into serving dishes or bowls.

Variation
Deviled Nuts: Add 1 teaspoon red (cayenne) pepper with the salt.

Cream Cheese Stuffed Dates

1 (8-oz.) carton whipped cream cheese
1 lb. pitted dates (about 60)

1. Spoon cream cheese into a pastry bag fitted with a star tip. Pipe cream cheese into dates.
2. Insert wooden picks for easier eating. Makes about 60 appetizers.

Variations
Substitute pitted prunes or seedless grapes for dates. To fill grapes, cut grapes in half; pipe cheese on 1/2 of grapes halves. Top with remaining halves.

Basic Cheese Pastry

1-1/2 cups all-purpose flour
1/4 teaspoon salt
1/4 teaspoon paprika
3/4 cup butter or margarine
1 cup shredded Cheddar cheese (4 oz.), room
temperature

Cheese pastry can be used for all types of savory tartlets and canapés. For small items, there is no need to add a liquid. The pastry will be delightfully short in texture. If a more pronounced cheese flavor is desired, use half Cheddar and half Parmesan cheese.

1. Sift flour, salt and paprika into a medium bowl. With a pastry blender or 2 knives, cut in butter or margarine until mixture resembles coarse bread crumbs; stir in cheese.
2. Knead lightly until dough forms a smooth ball. If dough is too soft to handle, wrap in plastic wrap and refrigerate 20 to 30 minutes before using. Makes enough dough for about 48 small pastries.

Variation
Cheese pastry can also be used for a pie crust. Add a little water or egg yolk to the basic recipe for easier handling.

Clockwise from left: Shrimp-Filled Pastries, Cheese-Filled Pastries, Pâté-Filled Pastries, Bouchées

Nutty Cheese Bites

1 recipe Basic Cheese Pastry, opposite
1 egg, beaten
About 48 blanched almonds, walnuts or hazelnuts

1. Preheat oven to 400F (205C). Grease a baking sheet. On a lightly floured board, roll out pastry to 1/4 inch thick; cut into 1-inch rounds, squares and diamonds. Place on greased baking sheet; brush with beaten egg. Place 1 nut on each pastry.
2. Bake in preheated oven 10 to 15 minutes or until golden brown. Remove from baking sheet; cool on a wire rack. These can be frozen or stored up to 10 days in an airtight container. Makes about 48 pastries.

Bouchées

1/2 (17-1/4-oz.) pkg. frozen puff pastry, thawed
1 egg, beaten

Ham Filling:
5 tablespoons butter or margarine
4 oz. mushrooms, chopped
3 tablespoons all-purpose flour
1 cup chicken stock
2 cups finely chopped cooked ham (about 8 oz.)
Dash of hot-pepper sauce
Freshly ground white pepper to taste

1. Preheat oven to 425F (220C).
2. Unfold pastry sheet on a lightly floured board. Roll out pastry to 1/4 inch thick. Cut into circles with a 1-1/2-inch round cutter. Place circles on an ungreased baking sheet; brush with beaten egg. Mark center of each circle with a 1-inch round cutter, without cutting through pastry.
3. Bake in preheated oven 10 to 15 minutes or until puffed, crisp and golden.
4. Remove pastry shells from baking sheet; let cool slightly. Remove tops with a sharp knife and reserve. Scoop out any soft pastry with a teaspoon. Empty shells keep up to 10 days in an airtight container. Reheat before using.
5. To make filling, melt 1 tablespoon butter or margarine in a medium skillet over medium heat. Add mushrooms; sauté until limp, about 3 minutes. Set aside.
6. Melt remaining 4 tablespoons butter or margarine in a medium saucepan over medium heat. Stir in flour; cook, stirring, 2 minutes. Slowly stir in stock; cook until thickened, stirring constantly. Stir in sautéed mushrooms, ham, hot-pepper sauce and pepper. Fill shells with ham mixture; replace lids. Makes about 60 appetizers.

Shrimp-Filled Pastries

1/2 recipe Basic Cheese Pastry, opposite
3 tablespoons butter or margarine
3 tablespoons all-purpose flour
1-1/4 cups milk
1/2 teaspoon tomato paste
Salt to taste
Freshly ground white pepper to taste
8 oz. peeled, cooked small shrimp

To garnish:
Small parsley sprigs

1. Preheat oven to 400F (205C).
2. On a lightly floured board, roll out pastry to about 1/8 inch thick. Cut into rectangles to fit 24 (3-inch) boat-shaped tart pans. Prick bottoms with a fork. Place pans on a baking sheet.
3. Bake in a preheated oven 12 to 15 minutes or until light golden brown. Remove from pans; cool on a wire rack. Empty shells keep up to 10 days in an airtight container.
4. Melt butter or margarine in a small saucepan over medium heat. Stir in flour; cook, stirring, 2 minutes. Slowly stir in milk. Cook until thickened, stirring constantly. Stir in tomato paste, salt and pepper.
5. Reserve 12 whole shrimp for topping; chop remaining shrimp. Stir chopped shrimp into sauce. Fill each pastry shell with shrimp mixture. Cut reserved shrimp in half lengthwise. Top each filled pastry shell with half a shrimp and 1 small parsley sprig. Serve immediately or cover and refrigerate up to 6 hours. Makes about 24 appetizers.

Variations
Cheese-Filled Pastries: In a small bowl, beat 1/2 (8-oz.) package room temperature cream cheese with a little half and half. Spoon into a pastry bag fitted with a fluted tip; pipe filling into each pastry boat. Garnish with a little caviar.

Pâté-Filled Pastries: Press 4 ounces smooth liver pâté through a sieve into a small bowl. Stir in 2 teaspoons dry sherry. Spoon into a pastry bag fitted with a fluted tip; pipe filling into each pastry shell. Garnish with a slice of sweet dill pickle.

Stuffed Tomatoes

8 small tomatoes, cut in half
1 cup cottage cheese (8 oz.)
4 oz. cooked ham, finely chopped
1 teaspoon hot-pepper sauce or to taste
Salt to taste
Freshly ground pepper to taste

To garnish:
16 pitted green olives, cut in quarters

1. Carefully scoop out insides of tomatoes with a tea-spoon; reserve for use in soups or casseroles, if desired. Press cottage cheese through a sieve into a medium bowl.
2. Stir in ham and hot-pepper sauce. Season with salt and pepper. Spoon filling into tomato shells, mounding it in the center.
3. Arrange olive quarters like flower petals on top of cottage-cheese mixture. Cover and refrigerate up to 6 hours. Makes 16 tomato halves.

Stuffed Eggs

12 hard-cooked eggs, halved lengthwise
1/2 cup mayonnaise
1 tablespoon curry powder or to taste
Salt to taste
Freshly ground pepper to taste

To garnish:
About 8 pimento-stuffed olives, sliced

1. Scoop out egg yolks; place in a small bowl. Set egg whites aside. Mash yolks with a fork. Stir in mayonnaise, curry powder, salt and pepper.
2. Spoon into a pastry bag fitted with a fluted tip; pipe into reserved egg whites. Garnish each with 1 olive slice. Arrange on a serving platter.
3. Cover and refrigerate until served. Makes 24 halves.

Stuffed Mushrooms

36 large mushrooms
2 tablespoons butter or margarine
1 medium onion, finely chopped
1 cup fresh bread crumbs
4 oz. salami, finely chopped
2/3 cup grated Parmesan cheese (2 oz.)
Red (cayenne) pepper to taste

To garnish:
Finely chopped parsley

1. Position oven rack 4 to 6 inches from heat source. Preheat broiler.
2. Carefully break stems from caps; set stems aside. Melt 1 tablespoon butter or margarine in a large skillet. Add mushroom caps; cook 1 minute on each side.
3. Remove caps from skillet; set aside. Finely chop stems. Add remaining 1 tablespoon butter or margarine to skillet. Add chopped stems and onion; sauté until golden. Stir in bread crumbs.
4. Remove from heat; stir in salami. Spoon mixture into mushroom caps; sprinkle with cheese and red pepper. Place on an ungreased baking sheet.
5. Broil under preheated broiler until browned. Place on a platter; sprinkle with parsley. Makes 36 appetizers.

Cucumber Canoes

2 large cucumbers
Salt
6 oz. cooked shrimp, peeled, coarsely chopped
3 tablespoons mayonnaise
2 tablespoons chopped chives
Freshly ground pepper to taste

To garnish:
Red (cayenne) pepper

1. Trim off cucumber ends; score peel lengthwise with the prongs of a fork. Cut scored cucumbers in half lengthwise. Scoop out centers, leaving a 1/2-inch shell; place shells in a sieve.
2. Sprinkle cucumber shells with salt; drain 30 minutes. Rinse; pat dry with paper towels.
3. In a medium bowl, combine cucumber centers, shrimp, mayonnaise and chives. Season with salt and pepper.
4. Cut each cucumber half into about 6 pieces. Spoon filling into pieces; sprinkle each with a little red pepper. Makes 24 appetizers.

Clockwise from top: Stuffed Tomatoes; Celery Boats, page 52; Stuffed Eggs; Stuffed Mushrooms; Cucumber Canoes

Mortadella & Cheese Sandwiches

7 pumpernickel-bread slices
1/2 (8-oz.) pkg. cream cheese, room temperature
Salt to taste
Freshly ground white pepper to taste
28 thin slices mortadella or other cold cuts
28 pimento-stuffed olives, cut in halves

1. Spread pumpernickel slices with cream cheese. Cut into quarters. Season with salt and pepper.
2. Fold each mortadella slice in half, then cut almost in 2, cutting from outer edge to fold. Twist each half in opposite directions, then place diagonally on cream cheese, pressing down gently.
3. Arrange 1 olive half on each side of twisted mortadella. Makes 28 small sandwiches.

Tuna-Salad Sandwiches

9 large rye or whole-wheat bread slices, crusts removed
About 1/2 cup butter or margarine, room temperature
1 (12-1/2-oz.) can tuna packed in water, drained
3 tablespoons lemon juice
1/4 cup mayonnaise
Freshly ground pepper to taste

To garnish:
36 small sweet dill pickles, drained
6 hard-cooked eggs, sliced

1. Spread bread with butter or margarine; cut neatly into quarters.
2. In a medium bowl, combine tuna, lemon juice, mayonnaise and pepper. Spread on buttered bread, dividing mixture equally among quarters.
3. Make pickle fans. Slice each pickle into 4 lengthwise slices, starting at small end and cutting almost to large end. Spread out slices in a fan shape.
4. Top each sandwich with 1 egg slice and 1 pickle fan. Makes 36 small sandwiches.

Ham & Prune Sandwiches

5 large white-bread slices, crusts removed
About 1/4 butter or margarine, room temperature
8 oz. Danish ham slices
4 oz. cottage cheese with chives (1/2 cup)
Salt to taste
Freshly ground white pepper to taste
10 pitted prunes, halved
10 large orange slices, peeled

To garnish:
Watercress sprigs
Parsley sprigs

Danish open face sandwiches should be made as small as possible for easy eating. Arrange different toppings on the same platter for an eye-catching, mouth-watering spread. Use day-old bread or the toppings may not adhere to their bases. Secure toppings with a wooden pick, if necessary. Garnish the platter with watercress or parsley sprigs, if desired.

1. Spread bread with butter or margarine; cut each slice neatly into quarters with a sharp knife.
2. Cut ham into pieces the size of bread. Place 1 ham slice on each buttered bread piece. Put 1 heaping teaspoon cottage cheese on each ham slice; season with salt and pepper. Place 1 prune half on top of the cottage cheese; press down firmly.
3. Cut orange slices into quarters; arrange 2 quarters on opposite sides of each prune to form 'butterflies.' Makes 20 small sandwiches.

Celery Boats

Photo on page 51.

1 (8-oz.) pkg. cream cheese, room temperature
2 tablespoons anchovy paste
1/2 cup walnuts (2 oz.), finely chopped
Freshly ground pepper to taste
1 large head celery, stalks cut into 2-inch pieces

To garnish:
Paprika

1. In a medium bowl, combine cream cheese and anchovy paste. Stir in walnuts; season with pepper.
2. Fill celery pieces with mixture; sprinkle with paprika. Makes about 24 pieces.

Clockwise from left: Mortadella & Cheese Sandwiches, Ham & Prune Sandwiches, Tuna-Salad Sandwiches

Watercress Butter

1/4 cup butter or margarine, room temperature
1 bunch of watercress, finely chopped
Salt to taste

This butter is an attractive bright green in color.

1. In a small bowl, combine butter or margarine and watercress. Season with salt. Cover and refrigerate up to 24 hours, if desired.
2. Bring to room temperature before using. Makes about 1/2 cup.

Blue-Cheese Butter

1/4 cup butter or margarine, room temperature
2 oz. blue cheese, room temperature

1. In a small bowl, combine butter or margarine and cheese. Cover and refrigerate up to 24 hours, if desired.
2. Bring to room temperature before using. Makes about 1/2 cup.

Deviled Crab Dip

1-1/2 (8-oz.) pkgs. cream cheese, room temperature
4 to 6 tablespoons mayonnaise
2 teaspoons chili sauce
2 teaspoons Worcestershire sauce
Salt to taste
Freshly ground pepper to taste
1 medium cucumber, peeled, seeded, finely diced
Pinch of sugar
1 (6-oz.) pkg. frozen crabmeat, thawed, drained
1/4 teaspoon red (cayenne) pepper

This is a light creamy dip with a peppery bite. For a more pronounced crab flavor, double the quantity of crabmeat.

1. In a medium bowl, beat cream cheese and mayonnaise until soft and creamy. Stir in chili sauce and Worcestershire sauce. Season with salt and pepper.
2. Sprinkle diced cucumber with sugar; stir into cheese mixture. With your fingertips, pick through crabmeat, discarding bits of shell or cartilage. Fold crabmeat into cheese mixture. Spoon into a serving bowl; sprinkle with red pepper.
3. Cover and refrigerate until chilled or up to 8 hours before serving. Makes 10 servings.

Crudités

Aioli:
4 garlic cloves
2 egg yolks
1 cup olive oil
Salt to taste
Freshly ground pepper to taste
1 to 2 tablespoons white-wine vinegar

Crudités:
1 fennel head
Juice of 1/2 lemon
3 to 4 tomatoes, sliced
1/4 cucumber, cut into strips
1 celery heart, sliced
1/2 small cauliflower, cut into flowerets
2 zucchini, sliced
1 red bell pepper, sliced
1 green bell pepper, sliced

To garnish:
Chopped parsley
Chopped chives

Any fresh, crisp vegetables may be used.

1. To make the aioli, crush garlic in a medium bowl to a smooth paste. Add egg yolks, 1 at a time, beating well with a whisk.
2. Add oil, drop by drop until thickened, whisking constantly. Add remaining oil in a steady stream, whisking constantly. Add salt, pepper and vinegar to taste.
3. Cut fennel into quarters; toss in lemon juice. Arrange on a serving plate with remaining vegetables.
4. Spoon aioli into a serving bowl; sprinkle with parsley and chives. Serve with vegetables. Makes 4 to 6 servings.

Clockwise from top: Deviled Crab Dip, Raw vegetables, Hot Cheese & Herb Loaf, Blue-Cheese Dip

Blue-Cheese Dip

1/4 cup unsalted butter or margarine, room
   temperature
12 oz. blue cheese, room temperature
About 6 tablespoons milk
4 celery stalks, finely chopped
3/4 cup walnuts, finely chopped
Freshly ground pepper to taste

To serve:
Crisp raw vegetables, crackers or potato chips

1. In a small bowl, beat butter or margarine with an electric mixer until light and fluffy. Gradually beat in cheese, a little at a time. Gradually stir in milk until creamy.
2. Fold in 3/4 of the celery and 1/3 of the walnuts. Season with pepper. Spoon into a serving bowl. Combine remaining celery and walnuts; sprinkle over the top of dip.
3. Cover and refrigerate until chilled before serving. Serve with raw vegetables, crackers or potato chips. Makes 12 servings.

Hot Cheese & Herb Loaf

1 long French loaf
1/4 cup butter or margarine, room temperature
1 (8-oz.) pkg. cream cheese, room temperature
2 tablespoons finely chopped parsley
1 tablespoon dried leaf thyme, marjoram or basil
Salt to taste
Freshly ground pepper to taste

1. Preheat oven to 400F (205C). Cut bread in half lengthwise; spread cut surfaces with butter or margarine.
2. In a small bowl, beat cream cheese with herbs until thoroughly combined; season with salt and pepper. Spread cheese mixture on buttered bread, dividing it equally between each half.
3. Put loaf back together again; wrap in foil. Place directly on oven rack in preheated oven.
4. Bake 10 minutes. Open foil wrapping; bake 5 minutes or until loaf is crisp and cheese is hot. Remove from oven; discard foil.
5. Cut loaf into thick slices; place slices in a bread basket. Serve immediately. Makes 12 to 14 slices.

Hummus

1-1/4 cups dried garbanzo beans, soaked overnight,
   drained
1 onion, coarsely chopped
1 bay leaf
Juice of 1 lemon
2 garlic cloves, crushed
2 tablespoons olive oil
1-1/4 cups plain yogurt
1/2 teaspoon ground cumin
Salt to taste

To garnish:
Chopped parsley
Ripe olives

To serve:
Pita-bread rounds

It is best to cook beans, such as garbanzo beans, without using salt as it tends to toughen them if added at the beginning of the cooking time. Hummus is best made at least 24 hours in advance because it thickens on standing.

1. Put beans in a medium saucepan; cover with water. Add onion and bay leaf; bring to a boil. Reduce heat, cover and cook 1 to 1-1/2 hours, or until garbanzo beans are tender. Drain thoroughly; discard bay leaf.
2. In a blender or food processor fitted with the steel blade, process beans and onion pieces until smooth. Add lemon juice, garlic, oil, yogurt and cumin; process until combined. Season with salt.
3. Pour hummus into a serving bowl. Cover and refrigerate until chilled. To serve, garnish with parsley and olives. Serve with pita bread. Makes 8 to 10 servings.

Left to right: Hummus with pita bread, Marinated Mushrooms, Vegetable Terrine

Vegetable Terrine

4 tomatoes, thinly sliced
3 medium Russet potatoes, peeled, coarsely grated
1 (10-oz.) pkg. frozen chopped spinach, thawed, drained
4 oz. mushrooms, finely chopped
1 onion, grated
1/2 cup shredded Cheddar cheese (2 oz.)
1 tablespoon mixed dried herbs, such as parsley, basil, marjoram
2 eggs, beaten
2 tablespoons half and half
Salt to taste
Freshly ground pepper to taste

---

1. Preheat oven to 350F (175C). Grease bottom and side of a 3- to 4-cup round baking dish. Line bottom with tomato slices, reserving remaining slices for top.
2. In a medium bowl, combine potatoes, spinach, mushrooms, onion, cheese and herbs. Beat in eggs and half and half; season with salt and pepper.
3. Spoon mixture into prepared dish; arrange remaining tomato slices on top. Cover with foil or a lid.
4. Cook in preheated oven 1-1/2 hours. Cool slightly. Refrigerate overnight. Turn out of dish; cut into wedges. Makes 6 servings.

Marinated Mushrooms

1 tablespoon cider vinegar
1 tablespoon olive oil
1 tablespoon lemon juice
Few drops of Worcestershire sauce
2 tablespoons tomato paste
2 tablespoons water
2 teaspoons mixed dried herbs, such as parsley, basil, marjoram
1 small onion, grated
1 garlic clove, crushed
1 lb. mushrooms, sliced

To serve:
French bread

---

1. Place all ingredients except mushrooms in a large jar with a tight-fitting lid; shake well. Add mushrooms, pushing them down into liquid if necessary. Shake jar once again so mushrooms are coated with marinade.
2. Refrigerate 24 hours, shaking occasionally. Mushrooms will reduce in bulk during this time and produce some liquid. Serve chilled with French bread. Makes 6 servings.

Devils on Horseback

2 tablespoons butter or margarine
1 small onion, finely chopped
1 teaspoon rubbed sage
1 cup fresh bread crumbs
20 pitted prunes
10 bacon slices

1. Position oven rack 4 to 6 inches from heat source. Preheat broiler.
2. Melt butter or margarine in a small skillet. Add onion; sauté until soft. Stir in sage and bread crumbs. Stuff prunes with crumb mixture.
3. On a cutting board, stretch out bacon slices with the back of a knife, then cut each slice into 2 pieces. Wrap each stuffed prune in a piece of bacon; secure with a wooden pick. Place bacon rolls on a rack over a broiler pan.
4. Broil 4 to 5 minutes on each side or until bacon is crisp. Makes 20 appetizers.

Cheese Rounds

1 cup plus 2 tablespoons all-purpose flour
1/4 cup butter or margarine
1/2 cup shredded Cheddar cheese (2 oz.)
1 egg yolk
2 teaspoons cold water

1. Preheat oven to 400F (205C). Grease 2 baking sheets.
2. Sift flour into a bowl. With a pastry blender or 2 knives, cut in butter or margarine until mixture resembles coarse bread crumbs, then stir in cheese. Add egg yolk and water; mix to a firm dough.
3. Turn out on a lightly floured board, roll out to 1/4 inch thick. Cut into circles with a 1-1/2-inch round cutter. Place well apart on greased baking sheets.
4. Bake in preheated oven until golden brown, 10 minutes. Cool on a wire rack. Serve alone or with dips, or use as a base for savory spreads. Makes about 50.

Cheese Straws

3/4 cup all-purpose flour
Pinch of salt
Pinch of red (cayenne) pepper
1/4 cup butter or margarine
1/2 cup shredded Cheddar cheese (2 oz.)
1 egg yolk
2 teaspoons ketchup
2 to 3 teaspoons water

To glaze:
Beaten egg
Paprika

1. Preheat oven to 400F (205C). Grease 2 baking sheets.
2. Sift flour, salt and red pepper into a bowl. With a pastry blender or 2 knives, cut in butter or margarine until mixture resembles coarse bread crumbs. Stir in cheese. Add egg yolk, ketchup and enough water to make a stiff dough.
3. Turn out on a lightly floured board; roll out to a 1/4 inch thick rectangle. Brush with egg; sprinkle with paprika. Cut into 1-inch wide strips, then cut strips into 3-inch long pieces. Place on greased baking sheets.
4. Bake in preheated oven 10 to 15 minutes or until golden. Remove from baking sheets; cool on a wire rack. Arrange on a plate or stand in small cups to serve. Makes about 50.

Variation
Cut pastry into small circles with a 1-1/2-inch round cutter. Bake as above. Top cooled circles with cream cheese; sprinkle with poppy seeds.

Chive-Cheese Rounds

1/2 cup butter or margarine, room temperature
1/2 (8-oz.) pkg. cream cheese, room temperature
1 cup plus 2 tablespoons all-purpose flour
1 tablespoon chopped chives

1. Cream butter or margarine and cheese in a medium bowl until blended. Stir in flour and chives until combined. Shape into a ball; wrap in plastic wrap. Refrigerate at least 1 hour.
2. Preheat oven to 400F (205C). Grease 2 baking sheets.
3. On a lightly floured board, roll out dough to 1/4 inch thick. Cut into circles with a 1-1/2-inch round cutter. Place well apart on greased baking sheets.
4. Bake in preheated oven until golden brown, 10 minutes. Cool on a wire rack. Serve alone or with dips, or use as a base for savory spreads. Makes about 50.

Top to bottom: Spiced Almonds, page 60; Cheese Rounds with cream cheese; Chive-Cheese Rounds with Sage-Cream Cheese Spread; Devils on Horseback

Sage-Cream Cheese

1 (8-oz.) pkg. cream cheese, room temperature
1/2 teaspoon ground sage

1. In a small bowl, beat cream cheese and sage until combined.
2. Spoon into a pastry bag fitted with a rosette tip. Pipe on crackers or cheese pastries. Makes about 1-1/2 cups.

Caraway Spread

2 (8-oz.) pkgs. cream cheese, room temperature
1/2 teaspoon paprika
1/2 teaspoon caraway seeds
1/2 small onion, grated
1 small garlic clove, minced

To garnish:
1 teaspoon caraway seeds

1. In a medium bowl, beat all ingredients except 1 teaspoon caraway seeds until blended. Spoon into a serving bowl. Garnish with 1 teaspoon caraway seeds.
2. Cover and refrigerate up to 8 hours, if desired. Bring to room temperature before serving. Serve as a spread for crackers. Makes 10 to 12 servings.

Spiced Almonds

3 tablespoons sunflower oil
4 oz. sliced almonds (about 1 cup)
1/4 teaspoon salt
1 teaspoon curry powder

1. Heat oil in a medium skillet. Add almonds; sauté until golden brown, stirring.
2. Drain on paper towels, then place in a serving dish. Mix salt and curry powder together a small bowl; sprinkle over almonds; toss well to coat. Makes about 1 cup.

Olive-Bacon Rolls

30 large pimento-stuffed olives
2 cups shredded Cheddar cheese (8 oz.)
10 bacon slices

1. Position oven rack 4 to 6 inches from heat source. Preheat broiler.
2. Halve olives lengthwise; remove pimento strips. Finely chop pimento strips. In a medium bowl, combine chopped pimento and cheese. Stuff olive halves with cheese mixture; press olive halves back together.
3. On a cutting board, stretch out bacon slices with the back of a knife, then cut each slice into 3 pieces. Wrap each stuffed olive in a piece of bacon; secure with a wooden pick. Place bacon rolls on a rack over a broiler pan.
4. Broil 4 to 5 minutes on each side or until bacon is crisp. Makes 30 appetizers.

Tuna & Parmesan Puffs

1/2 cup butter or margarine
1 cup water
1 cup all-purpose flour, sifted
4 eggs
1/3 cup grated Parmesan cheese (1-oz.)

Filling:
1 (6-oz.) can tuna packed in water, drained
1 celery stalk, finely chopped
2 green onions, finely chopped
6 tablespoons mayonnaise

To garnish:
Parsley sprigs

1. Preheat oven to 400F (205C). Grease 2 baking sheets.
2. Combine butter or margarine and water in a heavy, medium saucepan; bring to a boil. Add flour all at once. Stir with a wooden spoon until dough forms a ball and comes away from side of pan.
3. Cool slightly. Beat in eggs, 1 at a time, beating well after each addition. Beat in cheese. Spoon mixture into a pastry bag fitted with a 1/2-inch plain tip. Pipe mounds, about 1-1/2 teaspoons, onto greased baking sheet, spacing them well apart.
4. Bake in preheated oven 12 to 15 minutes, until crisp and golden brown. Make a small slit in the side of each puff. Cool on a wire rack.
5. To make filling, in a small bowl, combine tuna, celery and onions. Stir in mayonnaise until combined. Spoon filling into cooled puffs. Arrange on a serving plate; garnish with parsley. Makes about 70 puffs.

Seeded Crackers

24 water crackers
1/4 cup butter or margarine, melted
Caraway, poppy or sesame seeds

1. Preheat oven to 350F (175C).
2. Brush 1 side of each cracker with butter or margarine. Sprinkle buttered side with caraway, poppy or sesame seeds; arrange crackers on ungreased baking sheets.
3. Bake in preheated oven 5 minutes or until crisp and hot. Serve immediately. Makes 24 crackers.

Clockwise from lower left: Seeded Crackers; Olive-Bacon Rolls; Martinis;
Deviled Nuts, page 47; Caraway Spread

Cheese Kabobs

8 oz. cooked smoked sausages
1 (8-oz.) can pineapple chunks (juice pack), drained
1/4 cucumber, cut into wedges
6 tomatoes, quartered
8 oz. Cheddar cheese, cubed
12 pitted dates, halved
1 grapefruit

1. Cut sausages in 1-inch pieces. Alternately thread sausage, pineapple, cucumber, tomatoes, cheese and dates onto 24 wooden skewers, using 1 of each.
2. Cut a slice from top of grapefruit to form a flat bottom. Place grapefruit, cut-side down, in the center of a plate. Insert skewers into grapefruit. Makes 24 kabobs.

Cheese & Nut Cubes

8 oz. cottage cheese with vegetables (1 cup)
1-1/2 cups shredded Cheddar cheese (6 oz.), room temperature
1 tablespoon Worcestershire sauce
3 green onions, finely chopped
Hot-pepper sauce
1 cup peanuts, finely chopped

1. Place cheeses in a medium bowl. Add Worcestershire sauce, onions and hot-pepper sauce to taste. Shape mixture into a 1-inch thick rectangle.
2. Wrap in plastic wrap; refrigerate until firm. Cut into 1-inch cubes. Spread peanuts in a shallow dish; coat cheese cubes with peanuts, pressing peanuts on with your fingertips.
3. Arrange on a serving plate; cover and refrigerate until served or up to 8 hours. Makes 8 to 10 servings.

Sausage Spears

1 (4-oz.) pkg. Boursin with garlic
1 (3-oz.) pkg. cream cheese, room temperature
20 thin slices mortadella or other cold cuts (about 8 oz.)
1/2 head of lettuce, shredded

1. Place cheeses in a small bowl; beat until blended. Divide mixture among mortadella slices. Roll up and secure each with a wooden pick.
2. Arrange lettuce on a serving plate; arrange rolls on lettuce. Makes 20 rolls.

Top to bottom: Cheese Kabobs, Cheese & Nut Cubes, Sausage Spears

Open-Face Sandwiches

Breads:
White bread
Whole-wheat bread
French bread
Rye bread
Crisp breads

Cheeses:
Cheddar
Edam
Gouda
Emmenthaler
Gruyère
Jarlsberg
Danish blue
Cottage cheese
Cream cheese

Toppings:
Sliced cold cuts
Sliced roast beef
Salami
Pâté

Cooked chicken
Sardines
Cooked shrimp
Pickled herring

Garnishes:
Onion slices
Chopped parsley
Cucumber twists and slices
Watercress sprigs
Tomato slices
Sweet dill pickle fans
Green or ripe olives
Hard-cooked egg slices
Red bell pepper slices
Green bell pepper slices
Shredded lettuce
Caviar
Orange slices
Grapes
Strawberries

Open-Face Sandwiches

These are ideal for small buffet parties. Each sandwich is a work of art. Assemble them in advance or let guests make their own. Make sure the bread base is firm enough to support the heavy topping without breaking apart. Large open-face sandwiches are traditionally eaten with knife and fork.

1. Use any of the suggested breads; spread with soft butter or margarine.
2. Place a slice of 1 of the cheeses on top. Select a topping and 1 or more of the garnishes to complement the cheese in flavor, but provide contrast in color.
3. Arrange the open sandwiches on platters.

Keeping Foods Fresh

Unusual buffet sandwiches or delicious, small canapés can make or ruin your reputation as a party giver. Use the following tips to prevent soggy or dry sandwiches.

If you need to make sandwiches or canapés ahead of time and you don't want them to be limp, choose toasted or crisp breads. Spread with soft butter, margarine or mayonnaise to protect the bread from moist fillings and toppings. Cover with plastic wrap or foil to prevent drying out.

Or you can spoon a thin layer of cool liquid aspic over each canapé or sandwich. The aspic will then set and prevent the topping from drying out.

Do not store strong-flavored fillings, such as tuna and onion, next to mild-flavored fillings because they will absorb the flavor and smell of the more pungent ones. Always tightly cover and store filling and prepared sandwiches or canapés in the refrigerator until served.

BEVERAGES

Parisian Blonde

1 jigger (3 tablespoons) whipping cream
1/2 teaspoon superfine sugar
1 jigger (3 tablespoons) orange Curaçao
1 jigger (3 tablespoons) dark rum
Crushed ice

To garnish:
Orange slices

---

1. Shake whipping cream, sugar, Curaçao, rum and ice in a cocktail shaker or a container with a tight-fitting lid.
2. Strain into a cocktail glass. Decorate with orange slices.
Makes 1 drink.

Bloody Mary

1 jigger (3 tablespoons) vodka
2 jiggers (6 tablespoons) tomato juice
1/3 jigger (1 tablespoon) lemon juice
1 dash of Worcestershire sauce
Salt to taste
Freshly ground pepper to taste
Crushed ice

To garnish:
Celery leaves

---

1. Shake vodka, tomato juice, lemon juice, Worcestershire sauce, salt, pepper and ice in a cocktail shaker or a container with a tight-fitting lid.
2. Strain into a wine glass. Garnish with celery leaves.
Makes 1 drink.

Left to right: Daiquiri, Little Devil, Piña Colada, Parisian Blonde

Cuba Libre

Ice cubes
2 jiggers (6 tablespoons) dark rum
Juice of 1/2 lime
Coca-Cola

To garnish:
Lime slices

1. Half fill a tall glass with ice cubes. Add rum and lime juice; stir well. Fill glass with Coca-Cola; stir.
2. Decorate with lime slices. Makes 1 drink.

Screwdriver

Ice cubes
2 jiggers (6 tablespoons) vodka
Orange juice

To garnish:
Orange slices

1. Half fill a tall glass with ice cubes. Pour vodka over ice. Fill with orange juice; stir well.
2. Decorate with orange slices. Makes 1 drink.

Piña Colada

3 jiggers (9 tablespoons) dark rum
1 jigger (3 tablespoons) coconut milk
3 tablespoons canned, crushed pineapple
2 cups crushed ice

1. Place rum, coconut milk, pineapple and ice in a blender; blend at high speed 30 seconds.
2. Strain into a tall glass; serve with a straw. Makes 1 drink.

Little Devil

1/2 jigger (1-1/2 tablespoons) lemon juice
1/2 jigger (1-1/2 tablespoons) Cointreau
1 jigger (3 tablespoons) dark rum
1 jigger (3 tablespoons) gin
Crushed ice

1. Shake lemon juice, Cointreau, rum, gin and ice in a cocktail shaker or a container with a tight-fitting lid.
2. Strain into a cocktail glass. Makes 1 drink.

Black Russian

Ice cubes
2 jiggers (6 tablespoons) vodka
1 jigger (3 tablespoons) Kahlua

1. Add 3 or 4 ice cubes to an old fashioned glass.
2. Pour vodka and Kahlua over ice cubes. Makes 1 drink.

Variations
White Russian: Make as directed above. Fill glass with whipping cream.
For a tall drink, make drink in a tall glass; fill with Coca-Cola.

Harvey Wallbanger

Ice cubes
1 jigger (3 tablespoons) vodka
4 jiggers (3/4 cup) orange juice
1/2 jigger (1-1/2 tablespoons) Galliano

1. Half fill a tall glass with ice cubes. Pour vodka and orange juice over ice; stir well.
2. Float Galliano on top by pouring it over the back of a teaspoon onto the vodka mixture. Makes 1 drink.

Daiquiri

Juice of 1/4 lemon or juice of 1/2 lime
2 jiggers (6 tablespoons) dark rum
1 teaspoon superfine sugar
Crushed ice

To garnish:
1 maraschino cherry

1. Shake lemon or lime juice, rum, sugar and ice in a cocktail shaker or a container with a tight-fitting lid.
2. Strain into a cocktail glass. Decorate with maraschino cherry. Makes 1 drink.

Claret Cup

1-1/3 jiggers (4 tablespoons) maraschino liqueur
2-1/3 jiggers (7 tablespoons) orange Curaçao
3 tablespoons superfine sugar
1 (750-ml.) bottle Claret
Ice cubes

To garnish:
Fruit in season, such as strawberries, oranges or
    peaches

1. Combine maraschino liqueur, Curaçao, sugar and Claret in a punch bowl. Add ice; stir until sugar is dissolved.
2. Decorate with fruit. Makes about 8 servings.

Peach Cup

2 large ripe peaches
2 (750-ml.) bottles Mosel wine, chilled
3 tablespoons superfine sugar
1 (750-ml.) bottle sparkling wine, chilled

1. Peel and chop peaches into a punch bowl. Pour 1 bottle Mosel over fruit. Add sugar; stir until dissolved. Cover and refrigerate 30 minutes.
2. Just before serving, add remaining bottle of Mosel and sparkling wine. Serve in wine glasses. Makes 10 to 12 servings.

Rhine Wine Cup

2 jiggers (6 tablespoons) maraschino liqueur
1 jigger (3 tablespoons) orange Curaçao
1-1/2 teaspoons superfine sugar
1 (750-ml.) bottle Rhine wine, chilled
Ice cubes

To garnish:
Fruit in season, such as strawberries, peaches or
    grapes

1. Combine maraschino liqueur, Curaçao, sugar and wine in a punch bowl. Add a few ice cubes; stir well.
2. Decorate with fruits. Serve in wine glasses or punch cups. Makes 6 to 8 servings.

Top to bottom: Claret Cup, Peach Cup, Rhine Wine Cup

Claret Punch

1 cup superfine sugar
3 (750-ml.) bottles Claret, chilled
1 cup lemon juice
2 jiggers (6 tablespoons) orange Curaçao
2 qts. carbonated mineral water, chilled
Ice cubes

To garnish:
Fruit in season, such as orange, strawberries, peaches

1. Combine sugar, Claret, lemon juice and Curaçao in a punch bowl. Stir gently until sugar is dissolved; add mineral water and ice.
2. Decorate with fruits. Serve in wine glasses. Makes 20 to 25 servings.

Sauterne Punch

1 cup superfine sugar
3 (750-ml.) bottles Sauterne, chilled
1 jigger (3 tablespoons) maraschino liqueur
1 jigger (3 tablespoons) orange Curaçao
1 jigger (3 tablespoons) Grand Marnier
Ice cubes

To garnish:
Fruit in season, such as strawberries, oranges,
    peaches

1. Combine sugar and Sauterne in a punch bowl; stir until sugar dissolves. Stir in remaining ingredients.
2. Add fruit. Serve in punch cups or wine glasses. Makes about 12 servings.

Variation
Substitute another sweet white wine for Sauterne.

Champagne Punch

1 cup superfine sugar
2 jiggers (6 tablespoons) brandy
2 jiggers (6 tablespoons) maraschino liqueur
2 jiggers (6 tablespoons) orange Curaçao
Ice cubes
3 (750-ml.) bottles Champagne
1 qt. carbonated mineral water

To garnish:
Fruit in season, such as peaches, strawberries

1. Combine sugar, brandy, maraschino liqueur and Curaçao in a large punch bowl; stir until sugar dissolves. Add ice, Champagne and mineral water. Stir gently.
2. Add fruit. Serve in punch cups or wine glasses. Makes 15 to 20 servings.

Left to right: Claret Punch, Sauterne Punch

Tequila Sunrise

Tequila Sunrise

1-2/3 jiggers (5 tablespoons) tequila
3-1/2 jiggers (10-1/2 tablespoons) orange juice
Ice cubes
1/2 jigger (1-1/2 tablespoons) grenadine

1. Stir tequila, orange juice and ice cubes in a small pitcher; strain into a tall glass.
2. Add ice cubes; slowly pour in grenadine. Let settle, but stir once before drinking. Makes 1 drink.

Margarita

Lemon slice or lime slice
Fine salt
1-1/2 jiggers (4-1/2 tablespoons) tequila
1/2 jigger (1-1/2 tablespoons) Cointreau
1 jigger (3 tablespoons) lemon juice or lime juice
Crushed ice

1. Moisten the rim of a cocktail glass with lemon or lime slice; dip in fine salt. Set glass aside.
2. Shake tequila, Cointreau, lemon juice or lime juice and ice in a cocktail shaker or a container with a tight-fitting lid. Strain into prepared glass. Makes 1 drink.

The Perfect Cup of Tea

To make a perfect cup of tea, follow these guidelines.

- Always use cold, freshly drawn water. Bring to a rapid boil.
- Preheat teapot by rinsing with hot water
- Place tea in preheated teapot. Use 1 teaspoon of loose tea or 1 regular teabag per cup. Loose tea can be added directly to the teapot, or place loose tea in a tea ball.
- Pour boiling water over tea, and steep for 3 to 5 minutes.
- If loose tea is used, strain as tea is poured into cups. If using tea ball or tea bags, remove before serving.
- Serve tea with sugar, lemon or milk. Never combine both lemon and milk or the tea will curdle.

San Francisco

1 jigger (3 tablespoons) orange juice
1 jigger (3 tablespoons) lemon juice
1 jigger (3 tablespoons) pineapple juice
1 jigger (3 tablespoons) grapefruit juice
2 dashes of grenadine
1 egg white
Crushed ice
Soda water

To garnish:
Orange or lemon slices

1. Shake orange juice, lemon juice, pineapple juice, grapefruit juice, grenadine, egg white and ice in a cocktail shaker or a container with a tight-fitting lid.
2. Strain into a wine glass. Fill glass with soda water. Decorate with orange or lemon slices. Serve with a straw. Makes 1 drink.

Corcovado

1 jigger (3 tablespoons) blue Curaçao
1 jigger (3 tablespoons) tequila
1 jigger (3 tablespoons) Drambuie
Crushed ice
Lemonade

To garnish:
Lemon slices or lime slices

1. Shake Curaçao, tequila, Drambuie and ice in a cocktail shaker or a container with a tight-fitting lid. Fill a tall glass with crushed ice.
2. Strain mixture over ice. Fill glass with lemonade; decorate with a lemon or lime slice. Serve with a straw. Makes 1 drink.

Tropical Cooler

2 cups orange juice
4 cups pineapple juice
6 cups lemonade
Crushed ice

1. Pour fruit juices into a large pitcher; stir to mix. Just before serving, stir in lemonade.
2. Pour into glasses containing crushed ice. Makes about 20 tall drinks.

Cranberry-Lemon Punch

1 (48-oz.) jar cranberry juice cocktail, chilled
1 (6-oz.) can frozen lemonade
1-1/2 cups cold water
1 (1-liter) bottle carbonated mineral water
Ice ring

1. In a punch bowl, stir cranberry cocktail, lemonade and water until lemonade melts.
2. Add mineral water and ice ring. Makes about 15 servings.

Variation
Use cran-raspberry juice cocktail. Top with 1 pint raspberry sherbert.

Appleade

2 large Golden Delicious apples
2 cups boiling water
1/2 teaspoon sugar

To serve:
Ice cubes
3 apples slices dipped in lemon juice

1. Finely chop apples; place in a medium, heatproof bowl. Pour boiling water over apples; add sugar. Let stand until cool; strain into a pitcher.
2. To serve, fill 3 tall tumblers with ice. Pour appleade over ice; decorate each glass with an apple slice. Serve with straws. Makes 3 servings.

Anita

1 jigger (3 tablespoons) orange juice
1 jigger (3 tablespoons) lemon juice
3 dashes of Angostura bitters
Crushed ice
Soda water

To garnish:
Lemon slices
Orange slices

1. Shake orange juice, lemon juice, bitters and ice in a cocktail shaker or a container with a tight-fitting lid.
2. Strain into a tall glass. Fill glass with soda water. Decorate with lemon and orange slices. Serve with a straw. Makes 1 drink.

Tenderberry

6 to 8 strawberries
1 jigger (3 tablespoons) grenadine
1 jigger (3 tablespoons) whipping cream
Crushed ice
Dry ginger ale

To garnish:
Ground ginger
1 strawberry, if desired

1. Place strawberries, grenadine, cream and a little ice in a blender; blend on high speed 30 seconds.
2. Pour into a tall glass. Add ginger ale and stir. Sprinkle a little ginger on top and decorate with a strawberry. Makes 1 drink.

Left to right: Appleade, Anita

Temperance Mocktail

2 jiggers (6 tablespoons) lemon juice
2 dashes of grenadine
1 egg yolk
Crushed ice

To garnish:
1 maraschino cherry

1. Shake lemon juice, grenadine, egg yolk and ice in a cocktail shaker or a container with a tight-fitting lid.
2. Strain into a cocktail glass. Decorate with maraschino cherry. Makes 1 drink.

Café Astoria

1 jigger (3 tablespoons) coffee syrup or coffee liqueur
2 jiggers (6 tablespoons) milk
1/3 jigger (1 tablespoon) pineapple juice
1/3 jigger (1 tablespoon) lemon juice
Crushed ice

1. Place coffee syrup or liqueur, milk, pineapple juice, lemon juice and a little ice in a blender; blend on high speed 30 seconds.
2. Pour into a cocktail glass. Makes 1 drink.

Carib Cream

1 small banana, chopped
1 jigger (3 tablespoons) lemon juice
1 jigger (3 tablespoons) milk
Crushed ice

To garnish:
1 teaspoon walnuts, finely chopped

1. Place banana, lemon juice, milk and a little ice in a blender; blend on high speed until smooth.
2. Pour into a cocktail glass; sprinkle walnuts on top just before serving. Makes 1 drink.

Left to right: Carib Cream, Café Astoria, Temperance Mocktail

Sweet Temptations

Chocolate Brazil Nuts

6 oz. milk chocolate, broken in pieces
6 oz. semisweet chocolate, broken in pieces
8 oz. shelled unsalted Brazil nuts

1. Line 2 baking sheets with waxed paper or foil. Melt chocolate as described opposite.
2. Using 2 forks, carefully dip each Brazil nut into chocolate, coating it completely. Allow any surplus chocolate to drain off against the side of the bowl before putting nut on a baking sheet lined with waxed paper or foil.
3. Let set before removing nuts from paper or foil. Keeps up to 4 weeks in an airtight container. Place in paper cups to serve. Makes about 1 pound.

Variations
Chocolate Almonds: Substitute blanched almonds for Brazil nuts.
Chocolate Cherries: Substitute candied cherries or well drained maraschino cherries for Brazil nuts.
Chocolate Hazelnuts: Substitute hazelnuts for Brazil nuts. Place hazelnuts in clusters of 3 on the baking sheet.

Chocolate Nut Clusters

8 oz. milk chocolate, broken in pieces
8 oz. semisweet chocolate, broken in pieces
1 lb. chopped nuts, such as pecans, almonds or
  cashews

Toasted hazelnuts and almonds are excellent coated with chocolate.

1. Line 2 baking sheets with waxed paper or foil. Melt chocolate as described above.
2. Stir in nuts until completely coated. Drop small spoonfuls on the paper or foil. Let stand until firm. Keeps up to 4 weeks in an airtight container. Place in paper cups to serve. Makes 36 to 40 clusters.

Chocolate for Dipping
Chocolates are great favorites with everyone and many can be easily made at home. The type of chocolate used is a personal choice. A good combination for dipping is equal proportions of milk chocolate and semisweet chocolate, either in squares or pieces. Chocolate coating is also easy to use.

The following chocolate recipes are simple ones. To melt chocolate, first chop it into small pieces. Place chocolate pieces in a bowl or the top of a double boiler. Place over hot, not boiling water, stirring occasionally, until chocolate melts—this takes 5 to 6 minutes. If chocolate becomes too hot, white streaks appear on the surface when it cools and these spoil the appearance of the finished chocolates. Once chocolate is melted, replace the hot water with cold water. Cool chocolate to 80F-85F (about 25C) for best results. Once chocolate has cooled, the cold water can be replaced with warm water to keep chocolate at the correct temperature.

Moisture or liquids will alter the texture of chocolate and make it thick and grainy. Be careful that no water or steam touches the chocolate. Chocolates made at home will not have the high gloss of professionally-dipped candies because of the different processes used in manufacture. Nonetheless, even with little or no experience you will be able to make some very attractive sweets.

Not all the melted chocolate can be used for dipping, because it becomes too shallow to coat large pieces. When this happens, stir in some chopped nuts or raisins. Drop by spoonfuls on waxed paper or foil to make clusters.

Truffles

8 oz. semisweet chocolate, broken in pieces
1/2 cup whipping cream
1 tablespoon rum
1 cup chocolate sprinkles

These can be served with after-dinner coffee.

1. Combine chocolate and cream in a small heavy saucepan over low heat, stirring constantly. Cool to lukewarm.
2. Stir in rum. Refrigerate until cooled to about 55F (13C). Beat with a mixer until mixture is creamy and light in color and texture. Refrigerate until firm enough to shape into balls; mixture will be slightly sticky.
3. Place chocolate sprinkles on a piece of waxed paper.

Using 2 teaspoons, divide chocolate mixture into about 30 pieces. Roll each 1 in chocolate sprinkles until completely coated.
4. Refrigerate until firm. Keeps up to 2 weeks in an airtight container. Place in paper cups to serve. Makes about 30 truffles.

Variations

Substitute unsweetened cocoa powder or sweetened cocoa drink mix for chocolate sprinkles.
Brandy Truffles: Substitute brandy for rum.
Coffee Truffles: Substitute coffee liqueur for rum.
Orange Truffles: Substitute orange juice for rum. Add finely grated peel of a small orange with orange juice.

Rum Balls

2 cups pound-cake crumbs
3/4 cup mixed candied fruits (4 oz.), finely chopped
1 tablespoon apricot jam
1 tablespoon rum or to taste
1 cup chocolate sprinkles

These are an ideal way of using leftover pound cake. They can be crumbled by hand, but will be finer and easier to mix evenly if the crumbs are made in a blender or food processor. For an extra special flavor use a selection of candied fruits, such as cherries, pineapple and a little preserved stem ginger.

1. Combine cake crumbs, fruit and apricot jam in a medium bowl. Stir in rum to taste. Stir until combined.
2. Place chocolate sprinkles on a piece of waxed paper. Roll small spoonfuls of mixture in chocolate sprinkles until coated. Keeps up to 10 days in an airtight container. Place in paper cups to serve. Makes 18 to 20.

Stuffed Dates

1 (7-oz.) pkg. marzipan or almond paste
1 teaspoon rum
Green food coloring, if desired
1/2 lb. dates (about 30)
Powdered sugar, sifted
Granulated sugar

Stuffed dates are quick to make and are popular served with coffee after a meal or as part of a assortment of sweets to offer guests.

1. In a small bowl, combine marzipan or almond paste, rum and food coloring, if desired. Blend until smooth.
2. Remove and discard pits from dates. Sprinkle a pastry board with a little powdered sugar; form marzipan mixture into a long sausage shape. Cut into as many pieces as there are dates.
3. Shape each piece into an oval; use to replace pit in each date. Roll stuffed dates in granulated sugar. Keeps up to 4 weeks in an airtight container. Place in paper cups to serve. Makes about 30.

Peppermint Creams

1 (1-lb.) box powdered sugar
1/4 teaspoon cream of tartar
2 tablespoons evaporated milk
1-1/2 teaspoons peppermint flavoring or 1/2 teaspoon peppermint extract
About 1/2 egg white (about 1 tablespoon)
Green food coloring, if desired

1. Sift powdered sugar and cream of tartar into a medium bowl. Add evaporated milk, peppermint flavoring or extract and egg white. Knead until pliable. If necessary, add a little more egg white, but keep paste firm enough to roll out easily.
2. Tint with food coloring, if desired. Peppermint creams look very attractive if colored pale green, or you may prefer to color half of mixture and leave remainder white. Add a drop of coloring at a time, then mix to get desired color.
3. Knead mixture on a board lightly dusted with powdered sugar. Roll out to 1/4 inch thick; cut into 1-inch circles. Place on waxed paper; let stand leave 24 hours to dry. Keeps up to 4 weeks in an airtight container. Makes 1 pound.

Chocolate Peppermint Creams

4 oz. semisweet chocolate, broken in pieces
1 recipe Peppermint Creams, opposite

To decorate:
Candy leaves
Candied violets

Candied mint leaves look best with green tinted peppermint creams and candied violets on the white ones.

1. Melt chocolate as described on page 72. Dip half of each peppermint cream into chocolate, then allow to drain for a second or two against side of pan.
2. Place coated peppermint creams on waxed paper to set. Place a small candy leaf or a small piece of candied violet in the center of each cream before chocolate sets. Keeps up to 4 weeks in an airtight container. Makes 1-1/4 pounds.

Genoise

4 eggs
3/4 cup sugar
1 teaspoon vanilla extract
3/4 cup all-purpose flour, sifted
3 tablespoons butter or margarine, melted

1. Preheat oven to 350F (175C). Grease a 13'' x 9'' baking pan. Line bottom of pan with waxed paper; grease paper. Dust paper and sides of pan with flour.
2. Beat eggs and sugar in a medium bowl over a pan of barely simmering water. Beat until thick and lemon-colored and mixture doubles in volume. Remove from heat; beat in vanilla.
3. Fold in flour in 2 batches. Fold in butter or margarine. Pour into prepared pan.
4. Bake in preheated oven 35 to 40 minutes or until center springs back when lightly pressed. Cool in pan on a wire rack 10 minutes. Remove from pan. Remove paper. Cool completely on rack. Makes 1 cake.

Glazed Fruit

2-1/2 cups sugar
1/2 cup water
1 lb. prepared mixed fruit, such as 8 oz. strawberries, 4 oz. grapes, 2 oranges, sectioned

These sugared fruits are delightful to eat and will certainly impress your guests. Cherries, tangerine sections or any other small firm dry fruits can also be used. Make them only one to two hours before you want to eat them, keep in a dry place as the sugar coating soon melts, particularly if the atmosphere is damp.

1. Oil a baking sheet. Combine sugar and water in a large, heavy saucepan over gentle heat. Stir until sugar dissolves. Bring to a boil without stirring. Cook until syrup reaches hard crack stage 300F (149C) or until a little syrup dropped into cold water separates into hard, brittle threads. Remove from heat.
2. Dip 2 forks in oil. Using coated forks, dip each piece of fruit into syrup to coat. Drain fruit for a few seconds, then place on oiled baking sheet until firm. If syrup becomes too stiff, return to heat for a short time.
3. Be *cautious* when dipping fruit; do not touch syrup with fingers as it is very hot and could cause a painful burn. If your hand is splashed, place it in cold water immediately.
4. Keeps up to 2 hours. Place in paper cups to serve. Makes about 50 pieces.

Chocolate Boxes

12 oz. semisweet chocolate, broken in pieces
1 baked Genoise, opposite
2-1/2 recipes Chocolate Buttercream, opposite

1. Melt chocolate in a small saucepan over very low heat, stirring constantly. Fasten 4 waxed paper or foil pieces to a work surface with tape. Pour melted chocolate onto the paper or foil pieces. Spread into 3 (9-inch) and 1 (12-inch) squares.
2. When set, trim off uneven edges and mark chocolate into 1-1/2-inch squares. There should be a total of 160 squares.
3. Trim edges from cake; cut into 5 (1-1/2-inch) strips. Cut each 1 in half horizontally and spread with a little buttercream. Reform strips and cut each 1 into 8 (1-1/2-inch) pieces. Spread a thin layer of buttercream over sides and top of each piece.
4. Taking care to handle chocolate as little as possible, press 1 square of chocolate against sides of each piece of sponge to form a neat box.
5. Put remaining buttercream in a pastry bag fitted with a rosette tip; pipe 3 lines of stars on top of each box. Will keep tightly wrapped up to 3 days. Makes 40.

Buttercream

3 tablespoons sugar
1/4 cup water
1 egg yolk
5 tablespoons unsalted butter or margarine, cut in small pieces

1. Place sugar and water in a small saucepan. Cook, stirring occasionally, until sugar dissolves. Bring to a boil. Boil until temperature reaches 230F (110C), without stirring.
2. While syrup is boiling, beat egg yolk in a small bowl. Quickly pour syrup into beaten egg yolk, beating constantly; beat until light and fluffy, about 5 minutes. Beat in butter or margarine, a piece at a time. If mixture curdles, beat in a little more butter or margarine.
3. Buttercream can be flavored to taste with liqueurs, extracts, grated lemon peel and orange or lemon juice or melted chocolate; see below. Use immediately or cover and refrigerate up to 2 days. To use after refrigerating, place in a bowl over warm water until it starts to soften, then beat until smooth. Makes about 1 cup.

Flavorings
Fruit-Flavored Buttercream: Add about 1 tablespoon liqueur or fruit juice and 1 teaspoon grated lemon or orange peel, or a few drops of extract for flavoring.
Chocolate Buttercream: Stir in 2 ounces melted, cooled chocolate.

Chocolate Boxes

Left to right: Glazed Fruit, Printainiers, Petits Fours

Printainiers

1 baked Genoise, page 76
2 recipes Buttercream, page 77
1 to 2 drops vanilla extract
Green and pink food coloring
2 teaspoons kirsch or few drops of almond extract

1. Trim edges from cake; cut lengthwise into 5 (1-1/2-inch) strips. Cut each strip in half lengthwise. Mix buttercream with kirsch or almond extract and spread a layer on each strip of sponge. Reform strips; place on a wire rack.
2. Divide remainder of buttercream into 3 equal portions. Flavor 1/3 with 1 to 2 drops vanilla, color 1/3 pale green and flavor with kirsch or a little almond extract. Color remaining 1/3 of buttercream pale pink.
3. Place each color buttercream in a separate pastry bag fitted with a rosette tip. Pipe a band of each color down the length of each strip, covering top of cake completely. Cut each strip into 8 equal pieces. Makes 40 pieces.

Petits Fours

1 baked Genoise, page 76
2 recipes Buttercream, page 77
1/4 cup kirsch or few drops of almond extract

Icing:
1 (1-lb.) box powdered sugar, sifted
3 to 4 tablespoons water
Green food coloring
20 blanched almonds

1. Trim edges from cake; cut lengthwise into 5 (1-1/2-inch) strips. Cut each strip in half lengthwise. Mix buttercream with kirsch or almond extract and spread a layer on each strip of sponge. Reform strips; place on a wire rack. Place a baking sheet under wire rack.

2. Put remaining buttercream in a pastry bag fitted with a 1/2-inch plain tip. Pipe a band of buttercream down the length of each strip. Refrigerate until firm.

3. In a medium bowl, combine powdered sugar and enough water to make a icing that can be poured. Add a little green food coloring. Stir well until smooth. Pour icing over each sponge strip, making certain sides as well as top are coated with icing. Put a plate under the wire tray to catch surplus icing. Reuse surplus if needed.

4. Split almonds in half; place 8 evenly on top of each band. Dip a knife into hot water and diagonally cut each strip between each nut. Best if served the same day. Makes about 40 pieces.

Petits Fours

A plate of small delicious looking petits fours is always a welcome addition to a party. They can be served at a wedding reception, and they will make a tea or morning coffee special. If you make two or three varieties, arrange them together on platters so that everyone can choose favorites.

Metric Chart

Comparison to Metric Measure

When You Know	Symbol	Multiply By	To Find	Symbol
teaspoons	tsp	5.0	milliliters	ml
tablespoons	tbsp	15.0	milliliters	ml
fluid ounces	fl. oz.	30.0	milliliters	ml
cups	c	0.24	liters	l
pints	pt.	0.47	liters	l

When You Know	Symbol	Multiply By	To Find	Symbol
quarts	qt.	0.95	liters	l
ounces	oz.	28.0	grams	g
pounds	lb.	0.45	kilograms	kg
Fahrenheit	F	5/9 (after subtracting 32)	Celsius	C

Liquid Measure to Milliliters

1/4 teaspoon	=	1.25 milliliters
1/2 teaspoon	=	2.5 milliliters
3/4 teaspoon	=	3.75 milliliters
1 teaspoon	=	5.0 milliliters
1-1/4 teaspoons	=	6.25 milliliters
1-1/2 teaspoons	=	7.5 milliliters
1-3/4 teaspoons	=	8.75 milliliters
2 teaspoons	=	10.0 milliliters
1 tablespoon	=	15.0 milliliters
2 tablespoons	=	30.0 milliliters

Fahrenheit to Celsius

F	C
200—205	95
220—225	105
245—250	120
275	135
300—305	150
325—330	165
345—350	175
370—375	190
400—405	205
425—430	220
445—450	230
470—475	245
500	260

Liquid Measure to Liters

1/4 cup	=	0.06 liters
1/2 cup	=	0.12 liters
3/4 cup	=	0.18 liters
1 cup	=	0.24 liters
1-1/4 cups	=	0.3 liters
1-1/2 cups	=	0.36 liters
2 cups	=	0.48 liters
2-1/2 cups	=	0.6 liters
3 cups	=	0.72 liters
3-1/2 cups	=	0.84 liters
4 cups	=	0.96 liters
4-1/2 cups	=	1.08 liters
5 cups	=	1.2 liters
5-1/2 cups	=	1.32 liters

INDEX